W9-AXZ-662

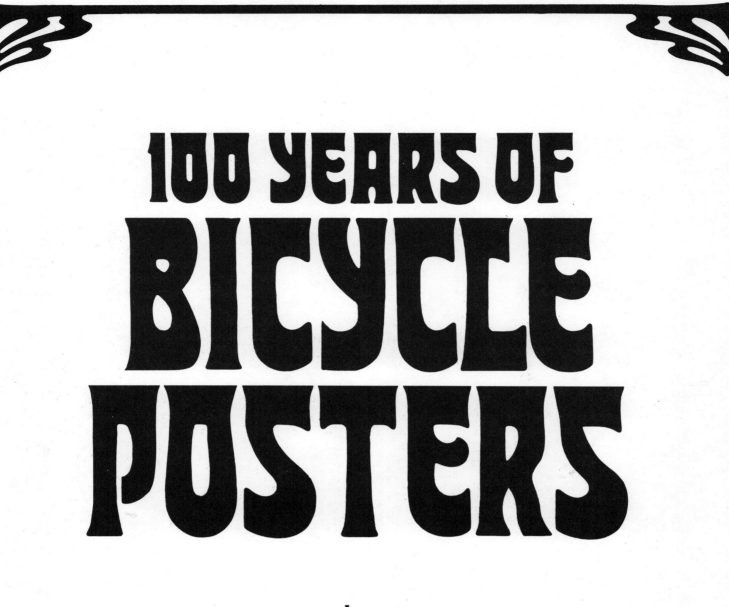

100 YEARS OF BICYCLE POSTERS

by
Jack Rennert

A Darien House Book

Harper & Row, Publishers
New York, Evanston, San Francisco, London

A DARIEN HOUSE BOOK

© COPYRIGHT 1973 DARIEN HOUSE, INC.
37 Riverside Drive, New York, New York 10023

All rights reserved.
No part of this book may be used or reproduced in any manner
whatsoever without written permission except in the case of
brief quotations embodied in critical articles and reviews. For
information address Harper & Row, Publishers, Inc., 10 East 53rd
Street, New York, N.Y. 10022. Published simultaneously in
Canada by Fitzhenry & Whiteside Limited, Toronto.

PRINTED IN THE UNITED STATES OF AMERICA.

FIRST EDITION

STANDARD BOOK NUMBER: 06-013533-6

LIBRARY OF CONGRESS CATALOG CARD NUMBER: 73-4118

Introduction

This year marks the one hundredth anniversary of two machines that have had a profound influence on us. It was roughly in 1872 that color lithography, which made colorful, pictorial posters possible, came into popular use; it was also about 1872 that the modern bicycle evolved. It is the coincidence of these two inventions — the modern bicycle and the modern poster — converging and maturing at about the same time, that interested me. It is this founding and parallel growth, as evidenced by the bicycle posters, that this book illustrates.

Both these inventions had their antecedents, of course. Briefly stated, lithography, the method of printing from a flat surface by purely chemical means, was founded by Aloys Senefelder in 1798. Until then, all printing was done by the relief method (letterpress, woodcut, etc.) or the intaglio or copperplate process, with lines etched directly on a plate. In the former, the ink adhered only to those parts of the surface that were raised; in the latter only the grooves held the ink, and the surface was wiped clean. But the lithographic or chemical process of printing was quite different. Explained Senefelder himself: "Here it does not matter whether the lines be engraved or elevated; but the lines and points to be printed ought to be covered with a liquid (or chalk), to which the ink (for printing) consisting of a homogeneous substance, must adhere, according to its chemical affinity and the laws of attraction, while at the same time, all those places which are to remain blank must possess the quality of repelling the color." In other words, grease and water won't mix. "Upon this experience rests the whole foundation of the new method of printing, the chemical method." Lithography at first used smooth, porous stones, later went to grained metal plates of zinc or aluminum, and still later curved these around a press cylinder to make today's high-speed offset-lithographs possible.

Although the first original color lithographs to be published can be traced to a series of architectural prints by Thomas Shotter Boys in 1839, this achievement lay largely dormant, and color printing in lithography was only revived through poster printing, with Jules Chéret leading the way. After a ten-year apprenticeship in a London printing shop, Chéret returned to Paris in 1866 to start his own plant, where he designed and issued large colorful posters the likes of which had never before been seen by the public. Chéret did not merely use separate plates, one for each final color tone, as Boys had done, but, by using overlapping color stones with varying degrees of color intensity, he was able to create an almost unlimited number of colors and shadings from three or four basic color stones. He established color lithography as an expressive medium for the artist and by using few stones on large presses (prints had previously required as many as fifty different plates for as many colors), he made the large, colorful poster economically feasible. With his design and printing of the "Bal Valentino" poster of 1872, the modern poster can be said to have been born.

The bicycle also had its earlier developments. From 1816, when Baron Karl von Drais first showed the "Hobby Horse," to later "Boneshakers" and Michaux's addition of pedals, there were many improvements that made possible the first modern bicycle. According to Arthur Judson Palmer, "Three years after the Phantom prototype appeared as an eye-opening advance in the evolution of the bicycle (wire spokes replacing the all-wood wheels in an 1869 patent of two Englishmen, Reynolds and Mays), the machine which most authorities consider the first real bicycle made its debut. This was the Ariel of 1872, built by Smith & Starley of England." *(Riding High, the Story of the Bicycle.* New York: E. P. Dutton. 1956.) James Starley's Ariel heralded the days of the "ordinary" or high-wheel bicycles. Although odd in appearance — the rider astride a high-wheel, with a much smaller stabilizing wheel with brakes in the rear — high speeds were obtained, and it created a revolution. In 1873, James Moore covered a little more than 14 miles in one hour on such an Ariel. The same year Rousseau won the Marseille-Avignon-Marseille race, covering 220 kilometers (about 137 miles), in 14 hours and 30 minutes.

Both the new lithographers and the new bicycle-makers were most impressed with their new machines and eager to show them off. There were bicycle shows and poster exhibitions. Bicycle manufacturers spoke only in superlatives and many of their posters proudly displayed their factories and machines. Likewise, poster printers bragged of their new-found invention. Camis, for instance, as if not to be outdone, would frequently put on the bicycle posters he printed "Les Plus Grandes Machines du Monde" (The world's largest presses). Although printers were required to put their names on all posters, they seem to have gone out of their way to make their names especially prominent on bicycle posters; Lemercier would often put his printing firm's name on three sides of the sheets.

One thing is certain: Poster artists were fascinated by the new bicycles, and bicycle manufacturers relied on the poster heavily for their marketing, both on the walls of the city and in the shops of their agents. By the turn of the century, more posters were created for bicycles than for any other product. Ernest Maindron, writing, in 1896, states that "the record for most illustrated posters belongs to the bicycle." He is not altogether happy about this development: "The bicycle, the tricycle, and the tandem increase in numbers daily, on our walls they occupy considerable space; on our roads they launch thousands of cyclists to whom we already owe an incalculable number of broken arms and legs. This is what we call the improvement of the race; the need for it is being felt. Cycling is in the process of balancing the budget and of eliminating the coachman." Fierce competition between bicycle firms created like competition between lithographers. In some cases, the accident of proximity might be interestingly exploited: Chéret's printing firm of Chaix, which produced hundreds of bicycle posters, was next door to the Clément bicycle factory (No. 18 and No. 20, Rue Brunel) in the 1880's. Could Clément have avoided printing more posters than almost any other bicycle firm?

Although specific comments are given for each poster reproduced in this book, a few general comments about this convergence of poster art and bicycle improvement, as illustrated by these posters, are appropriate.

First, we should note that there are few bicycle posters from the period 1872-1890. There are many reasons, but the chief one is that bicycles were extremely expensive before 1890, and the manufacturer was not interested in using the poster, a mass marketing tool, to reach the select few. Bicycles then cost $300 to $500 each, and if we use a multiple of 8, as is usually done to relate 1880 prices to current values, it would make these machines worth $2,400 to $4,000 each today. There were, instead, elaborately designed bicycle catalogues and advertisements in select periodicals, but few posters to cater to the general public appeared.

Also, it should be remembered that from 1871 to 1880, war stopped all bicycle production in France, and with defeat in the Franco-Prussian War and the collapse of the Second Empire, many French bicycle firms also folded. Michaux's plant was converted to war use and the large bicycle factory of the Parisienne Company (Olivier Frères) became a leading facility for the manufacture and storage of war supplies.

The second generalization to be drawn from a look at these posters is that, prior to 1900, they seem quite wild and extreme, in both their claims and their designs. Here we should remember what a revolutionary instrument the bicycle must have seemed a hundred years ago. Not only was it the fastest means of transportation available to a city dweller, it also had a tremendous liberating effect on him; it allowed him to leave the city or other environs bounded by his home and livelihood and reach out to new lands and horizons, both geographically and socially. And in this latter aspect, the bicycle was a truly liberating instrument, especially as it affected women.

And this brings us to a third observation about these posters: Women abound. Now the easiest explanation is that sex sells, then as now. But to women, especially, the bicycle, in its freedom of movement, of association, and of dress, was a significant and highly liberating instrument. And by picturing women, the manufacturer also implied ease of handling as well as the fact that "femininity" was not lost, as some charged, but increased by the riding of a bicycle. And so women were not only portrayed but were idealized in many of these posters. They could be free *and* feminine.

This brings us to another interesting common denominator at the turn of the century: the many allegorical and mythological figures to be seen on these posters. Most poster artists at the time had classical training, and the academicians reigned. It was the time of the *pompier,* and of gods and goddesses, and although posterists twisted these symbols to their commercial needs, they still had to use these popular motifs of the day to reach the public.

It is really the liberating influence of the bicycle that seems to have interested artists most. For it is ironic that although posterists were obviously fascinated by the bicycle, it was not the technical aspects, but the speed and freedom it afforded the rider — and the poster artist — that captured their fancy. Many of the posters here show the bicycle either badly drawn or largely hidden or even non-existent. The artist had respect for what the bicycle could do and little interest in how it worked. He sought the mood, not the machine. As frequently noted in the comments to these posters, bicycle spokes proved especially bothersome and were thus largely ignored. Only in the post-1910 posters is the frame and form of the bicycle itself seen as having a functional, usable design element for the poster artist.

Also apparent is that the international or multinational corporation we think of as today's corporate model, was in fact quite advanced in the bicycle industry at the turn of the century. I have not listed the posters by country of origin because that would be a difficult thing to do. How does one list a poster designed by a Czech artist and printed by a Parisian printer for the French agent of an American bicycle company, half of whose parts were manufactured in England? As these posters reveal, bicycle manufacturers had distributors or agents in several foreign countries; the bottom of the poster would be left blank for their imprinting or simply contain the words "Représenté par:", to be filled in later.

And how should we judge these posters as poster art? I feel they are among the best and liveliest examples of this medium. But let the reader judge for himself. As a guide, he might use this set of criteria, written by a poster artist and historian, W. S. Rogers. Writing in the "London Journal of the Royal Society of Arts" in 1914, Rogers indicated some of the functions and essentials of the poster: "(1) The pictorial poster must contain a good idea, original or originally expressed . . . (2) The poster must be simple and broad in treatment. (3) It must conform to the rules of pictorial composition. (4) It must be well drawn and well reproduced. (5) It must deliver its message with no uncertain voice, and if possible, without the help of explanatory lettering, or with very little. (6) It must be striking in colour scheme." He goes on to indicate that "even when all these conditions are satisfied, the poster may fail to achieve its purpose, for lack of some special quality that may be humour, beauty, grotesquerie, or other subtle factor calculated to appeal to the multitude which ultimately decides its value to the advertiser." Other desirable qualities of the pictorial poster he finds essential but more difficult and subtle to explain. One such quality he terms "the carrying force" of the poster and defines it as "that quality which would compel a man to cross the road to see what it is all about," indicating that "such a quality is more likely to be attained by the use of a simple colour scheme of vivid contrasts in large masses of flat colour, than by a more elaborate rendering of the subject." Now that the poster has the attention of the spectator, "it must interest him, or he will not read its message, hence the value of humor." Another quality of poster art he calls "reticence" and defines it thus: "It consists in leaving something for the imagination of the spectator to supply. The public likes a problem picture, and is ever ready to exercise its ingenuity in providing the missing link in the story." These are difficult standards to meet; I think a good many posters here will pass the test.

There were other historic connections between bicycles and posters. The 1890's saw the height of both poster craze and the bicycle craze. And there is evidence of this convergence again today. A poster craze, largely dominated by photo blow-ups and psychedelic splashings began in the mid 1960's, just as the bicycle craze, in the United States at least, began to gather steam. Pedal power reached its height in 1972, when total sales in the United States reached over 13,000,000 bicycles — for the first time outselling automobiles. And while it would be pleasant to report that this renaissance of the bicycle has met with a new wave of bicycle posters, this is unfortunately not the case. Several reasons may be advanced, none of which are individually quite satisfactory. In the first place, the more than 100 current posters we received after writing to more than 800 individual bicycle firms throughout the world had virtually one thing in common. They were all photographic, showing a beautiful girl (or couple) standing in front of or riding upon that firm's newest bicycle model. (Posters *96* and *112* are the most interesting of many such samples in this group.) Although I am not one who believes that photography leaves poster art totally bereft of creative spark or interest, it does make it all too easy to pass off a blow up of a catalogue page or magazine advertisement as a poster; few such advertisements were created specifically for poster use. Another problem has been that, although fierce competition in the 1890's resulted in the poster's use as the principal means of advertising, today there are competing media, notably television; in addition, the fact that demand has outstripped supply in the past few years means that bicycle manufacturers don't need to spend so much money on advertising. When I approached America's leading manufacturer of bicycles and suggested that he sponsor a worldwide competition of posters, as the Pope Company had done in 1896, he was aghast at the suggestion: His plant was already working around the clock, at full capacity, and he was still six months behind in meeting orders. The last thing he wanted was to advertise; at this stage, more orders would only mean alienating more people. To this must be added the sad fact that, especially in the United States, the opportunities for public posting remain quite meager.

However, as the bicycle becomes a principal tool in the fight against air pollution, a cause that artists have long recognized and espoused, and as a stabilized market creates greater competition among firms, and finally, as the subway systems and kiosks increase in the United States, let us hope that the poster will come into its own and that fine bicycle posters will again be produced and decorate our cities. If this book serves as a catalyst or inspiration, to bicycle manufacturers and to artists, then it will have served a very useful purpose indeed.

Some Notes on the Posters

Although explanatory text is provided for each of the 96 posters reproduced in this book, let me state at the outset that one need not feel guilty about skipping this verbiage and going right to the good parts — the pictures. Nothing is more boring than descriptions of works of art, and rhapsodizing over poster art can be especially ludicrous. So if you wish, read. If not, look and enjoy.

The posters in this collection have been arranged in no particular order other than roughly chronological. To keep things simple, the page and illustration numbers are identical. Size is given to nearest inch and nearest centimeter, width precedes height. (I realize that most art books do the reverse, but I have found that if you hand out rulers, 7 out of 10 people will measure the width of a poster first; and posters being the people's art, it is important to keep the people's habits in mind.) Where the artist is unknown to me (and to the museum curators and collectors consulted), I have indicated "Unknown." I realize this also goes against the practice of listing them as "Anonymous." But there are two things that bother me about "Anonymous": In the first place, it removes part of the sting of ignorance or laziness from the author who — this one not excepted — might have been able to identify the designer of the work had he been more industrious. Secondly, at a time when many posters are produced by large corporations and their advertising agencies, there is a tendency to list the creator as "Anonymous," as though some designer, photographer or art director did not have a personal hand in its creation. Until someone shows me a purely computer-designed poster, I'll stay with "Unknown." (Hopefully, some more knowledgeable reader will fill in some of the blanks so that future editions of this book can be more accurate.) The method of reproduction is commented on only where it is relevant or adds to our understanding of the posters; with the exception of two silk-screened illustrations, all posters were produced lithographically, whether by stone or photo-offset.

The process of selection is always difficult, but here it was often quite painful. In the first place, the selection was limited to posters advertising bicycles or bicycle tires, and posters for bicycle shows, exhibitions, races and "vélodromes." This unfortunately, but necessarily, omits some fine posters on subjects more peripheral to bicycles, such as posters for bicycle journals (Chesworth's poster for "The King of the Road" or Misti's for "Le Vélo," to name just two of more than a hundred of such examples), or solely motorcycle posters (such as Steinlen's Motocycles Comiot poster). One has to draw the line somewhere.

Having narrowed the field to the above subjects, I further limited myself by a personal desire to include only posters that would be photographed especially for this book from the original posters themselves, and with only three exceptions (photographs of poster reproductions) this was achieved; not a single poster was reproduced from a book or catalogue, as is too frequently the case. This unfortunately meant that some posters I wanted could not be included in the book — Chéret's poster for Cleveland Bicycles or Maxfield Parrish's winning 1896 design for the Pope Company's poster exhibition, or Jean Mercier's Olympique Cycles poster of 1924, among others — because the originals could not be located by presstime. The final selection was made from almost 1,000 bicycle posters viewed and photographed in leading museums and collections and received from many bicycle manufacturers throughout the world. In selecting the final 96 samples shown here, the decision was not only difficult but obviously personal as well. I have tried to show the diversity of design approaches, the possibilities of the lithographic medium, the best examples of poster art, and those with some historic and social interest as well. I wanted the viewer to have an appreciation of the times as well as the artists. Wherever possible, preference was given to previously unpublished works. I enjoyed looking at — and in some cases living with — these posters. I hope the reader is able to share some of that enjoyment with me. Posters please:

17
Artist: Unknown. Product: Howe Bicycles. Year: c. 1878. Size: 39 x 59 in. / 100 x 149 cm. Courtesy: Bibliothèque Nationale, Paris.

This is one of the earliest bicycle posters on record and, of course, should more properly be called a tricycle poster. This poster, for Howe's French agent, shows an improvement by James Starley over his previous Coventry Lever tricycle, and it marks the first appearance of one of Starley's most important inventions, the differential axle. The importance of the differential gear is the additional balance and mobility it gives: It spreads the pedaling effort equally between the wheels on each side but allows these wheels to rotate at slightly different speeds when turning corners.

In 1878 Starley took a train, like the one in the background of this poster, from Coventry to London, to take out yet another patent for his new tricycle, featuring the differential gear, which became known as the Royal Salvo Quad: "Royal" because in 1881 Queen Victoria ordered two such tricycles, and "Quad" because greater stability was given by the tiny wheel which can be seen in the rear. Safety, stability, and ease of handling were the alleged advantages of the tricycles over the previous two-wheelers, and it became especially fashionable for women and elderly gentlemen.

The Howe Machine Company was best known for its high-wheeler or "Ordinary," called the Howe Spider, which featured Starley's radial spokes. This was the most popular vehicle of the day until displaced by the tricycle in the 1880's. However, the introduction of the "safety" bicycle in the 1880's — a lower vehicle driven by a chain in the back of two equal-sized wheels — to which pneumatic tires were added in the 1890's, brought the two-wheeler back in vogue and doomed the tricycle.

As with so many other posters in this collection, the country of manufacture is not necessarily the country of publication. This poster was printed in Paris by the lithographer F. Appel, who also printed a poster for a similar tricycle for Clément & Cie. Also typical is the juxtaposition — and thereby the favorable allusion — to the fastest known method of transportation to date, the railroad, although in this poster the element of comfort seems as important as that of speed. An interesting design element here is the parallel motion of the train's smoke and the gentleman rider's windswept scarf around his hat. (And to the right of that is another familiar element, not meant as part of the design, a tear along the fold of the poster which shows as a horizontal streak.) In the United States, posters for an almost identical machine, the Columbia tricycle, were published in 1884 by the Pope Manufacturing Company of Boston.

18
Artist: Abel Truchet. Product: Morel Tires. Year: c. 1898. Size 24 x 31 in. / 62 x 80 cm. Courtesy: Bibliothèque Nationale, Paris.

This poster was printed by one of the great lithographers of the day, Edward Ancourt, who is best known for his posters for Lautrec and Bonnard. The influence of the latter artist can be seen in the head of the baby. Truchet was one of the organizers of the "La Vâchalcade" spectacle, an effort by the successful writers and artists of Montmartre to collect money for their more needy compatriots.

The translation of the text: "Try Morel tires on your bikes — they go on and off instantly."

And at the bottom is this conversation between the two youngsters:

— "Listen, George, put my tire on quickly; here comes mom and dad."

— "Don't be afraid, my little Riri, it's done."

19
Artist: Frederick Winthrop Ramsdell. Product: American Crescent Cycles. Year: 1899. Size: 42 x 63 in. / 106 x 160 cm. Courtesy: Athena Reproductions, London.

An American bicycle (manufactured by Western Wheel Works of Chicago), designed by an American artist, but printed by France's foremost lithographer, Chaix. Ramsdell studied in New York and Paris. Portraiture and landscape were his specialty, as can be seen in this typical "symboliste" style poster. Flowing hair and flowers were, of course, the trademark of the Art Nouveau style, but here they have been refined and given functional purpose as well as decorative motif: The sweeping and windswept gown, hair and flowers combine to give this poster a feeling of movement and yet also of grace and serenity, although the girl herself is not even seated on the barely noticed bicycle. It is a mood meant to complement the product and highlight its quality, and these ends are brilliantly achieved.

20
Artist: Jean-Louis Forain (1852-1931). Event: Second Bicycle Show. Year: 1894. Size: 82 x 35 in./ 208 x 89 cm. Courtesy: Bibliothèque Nationale, Paris.

This poster announces the second bicycle show, to be held in October 1894, at the Palace of Industry in Paris. These exhibitions of bicycles and bicycle parts were an important element in the marketing of bicycles as well as a major social event. All the manufacturers showed their latest models, as did the prospective customers. The first "Salon" was held in January, the second in October of 1894. Forain was a prolific painter and lithographer, but is best known for his book designs and numerous illustrations for leading French periodicals such as *Le Rire, Courrier Français, Vie Parisienne, Echo de Paris,* and others. He produced few posters, but this one is widely — and correctly — regarded as his finest. It was also produced in a smaller format of 43 by 17.5 inches (109 by 44 cm.).

21
Artist: Eugène-Samuel Grasset (1841-1917). Product: Georges Richard Bicycles and Automobiles. Year: 1897. Size: 58 x 43 in. / 147 x 109 cm. Courtesy: Private Collection.

Grasset was one of the leaders of the Art Nouveau school of design and one of its greatest theoreticians as well as practitioners. He was active in the design of posters, books, furniture, paintings, buildings, stained-glass windows, clothing, typography, etc. One of his motivating ideas was that art should "intrude" everywhere. ("L'Art ne doit pas avoir se préjugés, il doit tenir à s'introduire partout.") He wrote books on composition and design, including "La plante et son application ornamentale." (The plant and its decorative uses.) He insisted on a return to the direct study of nature in order to find new ornamental motifs, stylizing natural elements and still remaining true to the character of the subject portrayed. Here he gets an assist from the manufacturer: The text to the left proclaims the four-leaf clover to be the brand symbol of Georges Richard bicycles. This poster is the perfect fusion and summation of his life's work. It is also his last poster.

As with Ramsdell's poster for American Crescent *(19)* the mood is paramount. In common with that poster is the fact that the woman is standing next to a man's bicycle, although women's bicycles, with depressed top tubes, were being manufactured at the time. One can only speculate: Is this because far more men's bikes were being sold? Or, are we to imagine that the lady is holding the bicycle for a male companion, present or anticipated, but definitely off-stage (or off-poster)? The twilight effect adds to the romance. But the superiority of the Grasset poster is quite evident, especially in the fine integration of type and design.

Malherbe, the lithographer who did so much to encourage young artists to explore the possibilities of color lithography, printed this and all other posters created by Grasset.

22
Artist: Deville. Product: Aluminum Bicycles. Year: 1895. Size: 35 x 50 in. / 88 x 128 cm. Courtesy: Bibliothèque Nationale, Paris.

This "aluminum-made" bicycle's lightness is made evident by the ease by which the young lady lifts the new bicycle. If her colleague has a surprised expression, it should be remembered that bicycles of that time weighed as much as 60 pounds each and lightness became a competitive edge in a highly competitive business. This one, using tubular aluminum construction, weighed about 20 pounds. Look ma, one hand only!

23
Artist: Eugène Ogé. Product: Snell American Bicycles. Year: c. 1897. Size 20 x 32 in. / 51 x 72 cm. Courtesy: Galerie Documents, Paris.

With Spaulding and Pope leading the way, the American bicycle market became saturated in the 1890's, and in 1896 and 1897 American brands began to flood the European market. This invasion is depicted in this poster by Ogé, a designer and lithographer who had attached himself to one of France's leading poster printers, Charles Verneau, best known for printing almost all of Steinlen's masterpieces. Ogé turned out many "anonymous" posters for Verneau, but did sign several, including other bicycle posters for L'Etoile Cycles and Vélodrome de l'Est. Maindron is full of praise for Verneau and his "collaborateur habituel" Ogé. Ogé, he states, "est certainement un lithographe de premier ordre, un artiste de grande valeur." How much of this comes through in this poster? His skill as a lithographer is seen in the way he can express his message although limited to two colors: black and red. The design, however, is more cartoon than poster, with the coachman being understandably disturbed by this new device which threatens his livelihood. An early kiosk appears in the rear, but this poster was meant for in-store use only.

24
Artist: Will H. Bradley (1868-1962). Product: Victor Bicycles. Year: 1899. Size: 39 x 62 in. / 100 x 158 cm. Courtesy: The SandyVal Graphics Ltd. Collection.

Bradley was certainly America's best-known and most prolific poster artist, its very own "Chéret" — not in style so much as in popularity and output. And for style he was much influenced by the entire Art Nouveau school of design, but especially by the English artist Aubrey Beardsley. The poster craze came to the United States in the mid 1890's, and there were thousands of poster collectors and many poster publications. All leading bookstores sold the best of current advertising posters of the day, including the works of Lautrec, Cheret, Beardsley, Mucha, Grasset, and others, at prices ranging fom $1.00 to $6.00. (Brentano's bookstore in New York City, which sold a Chéret and Lautrec poster for $5.00 in 1896, is now selling these same posters for $1,000 to $5,000).

Bradley designed many magazine covers, especially for *The Inland Printer, Harper's Weekly, Harper's Bazaar,* and later, *The Chap-Book.* Many of these were enlarged into posters. He was a printer and quite familiar with typography as well, and in 1895 he opened the Wayside Press in Boston and published his own art magazine, *Bradley: His Book.* But design was his interest and printing only a "wayside," and he chose the dandelion leaf motif, seen here and in so many of his other works, "because the dandelion is a wayside growth." He designed many beautiful bicycle catalogues, including some for Columbia bicycles, as well as posters for the Springfield Bicycle Club *(57).* But his finest work was done for Victor. (See also *51*). The bottom banner was changed to meet the different marketing needs of Overman. In this case, there is a banner for their Italian agent. (Bradley later used the same design for a poster advertising the Bar-Lock Typewriter of London: The identical ladies seen in front and middle have hands on typewriter rather than bicycle handle; the ornate frame is unchanged.) After the turn of the century, Bradley became art editor of *Collier's* and *Good Housekeeping,* designed type faces, wrote a novel, and became involved in many facets of the Hearst organization, including art supervision of their motion pictures as well as their magazines.

Although Pope's "Columbia" — an "ordinary" bicycle with high front wheel and low rear wheel, weighing about 70 pounds and costing more than $300.00, launched the American bicycle industry in 1878, it was A. H. Overman's Victor Bicycles, beginning in 1887, with their two identical wheels and diamond frame construction, which started an American craze for the bicycle. By the time this poster was made, pneumatic tires, ball bearings and light tubular steel combined to make the bicycle so attractive and relatively inexpensive that there were about 4,000,000 cyclists in the United States, and over 500 bicycle shops to cater to them.

17

18

19

20

21

22

23

24
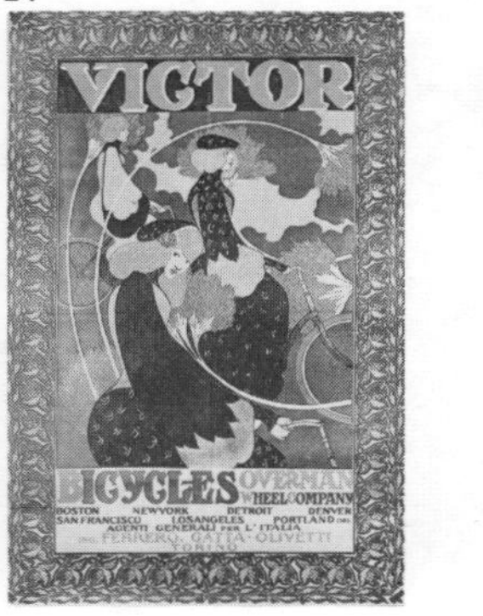

25
Artist: PAL (pseudonym for Jean de Paléologue, born 1855). Product: Falcon Bicycles. Year: c. 1895. Size: 41 x 56 in. / 104 x 142 cm. Courtesy: Private Collection.

Pal, who was born in Bucharest but studied art in London and Paris, created more bicycle posters than any other artist. He did posters for Déesse (*62*), for Whitworth, Cleveland, Liberator (*48*) Humber, Clément, Palais de Sport, and many more. The influence of the *pompier* artists was very strong, and Pal, like Lautrec and other poster artists influenced by their classical academic training, used classical symbols, such as goddesses, in their advertising. Women dominate his posters, and they tend to be much sexier than Chéret's girls.

Falcon and Bixton were the two French brands of the Franco-American Bicycle Company. Note that, as often, the spokes of the wheel presented too much of a design problem and were completely left out, here to indicate speed, no doubt, but elsewhere even when not in motion.

26
Artist: H. Gray (1858 -?) Product: Sirius Bicycles. Year: 1899. Size: 38 x 54 in. / 97 x 137 cm. Courtesy: Private Collection.

Here is the full flowering of the fin-de-siècle style and one of the best bicycle posters ever done. It is light, gay, colorful, bold, compelling; it expresses all the qualities of the bicycle also: so fast it can reach the stars, yet so light and feminine too. And Gray is not afraid to show the spokes; if the young lady is impervious to her robe being caught in them, why should *he* care? Gray probably ranks as one of the greatest unknown poster artists in history. Very little is known about him and almost every book on the subject of poster art is able to make it through to the last page without even mentioning his name. Most of his posters were done for the French railroads and the resort cities they served, but he also did one for the Barnum-Bailey circus tour in Paris as well as one for Gladiator automobiles and bicycles. Almost all these are quite forgettable. One exception, in addition to the one illustrated in this book, is a remarkable poster for Petrole Stella which has wild surrealistic qualities about it and is even sexier than the one shown here, since it reveals not only full breasts but navel as well. Yes, that was considered daring at that time. But that doesn't mean that Gray isn't good for something: At any gathering of poster freaks I've always been able to win a round of drinks by asking which poster artist brought the lowest price in the history of Sotheby sales? You guessed it; H. Gray, was had for two pounds, which is less than five dollars. Or, you can win as much as that by stumping your fellow collectors with the likes of: "If Forain did the famous poster for the Second Bicycle Show (*20*), who was the artist who did the poster for the First Bicycle Show?" Our friend Gray again. (That's a variation of "Who was the second man to walk on the moon?")

Although I have championed the work of this obscure artist for several years, I have been able to find very little about his life. Maindron tells us that he came to light as an illustrator for *Le Courrier Français* in 1884, and he also did some work for *Le Chat Noir*. In only one poster does he sign his first name, "Henry." So possibly he was originally English. But another clue contradicts this: The catalogue listing at the Victoria and Albert Museum in London states: "GRAY, Henri (or Grivois) (pseudonyms of Boulanger, —) (1858-?) French." The only interesting thing about this is that "Grivois," according to Larousse, means "Spicy, racy, licentious, broad, bawdy." Since that says it all, possibly I should stop investigating.

Sirius, by the way, was a German make, manufactured by Sirius Fahrrad-Werke GmbH of Nurnberg, but the brand name was sold in 1901 to Triumph Werke, also of Nurnberg.

27
Artist: Henri Thiriet. Product: Griffiths Bicycles. Year: 1898. Size: 37 x 51 in. / 94 x 130 cm. Courtesy: Bibliothèque des Arts Décoratifs, Paris.

Another fine example of Art Nouveau as expressed in a bicycle poster. Here, the young girl, whose purity and freshness are emphasized by the whiteness of her gown and the flowers she scatters, is contrasted to the elderly woman amidst briers. The bicycle thus connotes youth and a new mobility and freedom, not possible for the older generation, symbolized by the cane. Another Thiriet poster appears on page 56.

Beginning about 1890, the Avenue de la Grande Armée became known as "L'Avenue du Cycle," with more than twenty bicycle showrooms on that one street alone, including Couturier, Renard, Lonclas et Guibert, Larippe, Phebus, Peugeot, Clément, Dupressoir, Griffiths, Columbia, Waverley, and others.

28
Artist: Henri de Toulouse-Lautrec (1864-1901). Product: Simpson Chains. Year: 1896. Size: 45 x 39 in. / 124 x 89 cm. Courtesy: Bibliothèque Nationale, Paris.

If Chéret was the father of the poster, then Lautrec was its master. And although the former produced more than 1,300 different posters, the latter, in his brief life span, only produced 31 posters. Lautrec was an avid sports fan, and especially followed bicycle racing, having been introduced to the world of cycling by his friend Tristan Bernard, an impresario who was also sports director of the Buffalo Vélodrome (*54*) and the Vélodrome de la Seine. Although unable to ride a bicycle himself, Lautrec attended one of the Vélodromes each Sunday. Through Bernard, seen in the background with black hat and beard, he met Louis Bouglé, the French agent for Simpson chains, who had adopted the name Spoke. The first poster commissioned from Lautrec for "Cycle Michaël" was unacceptable, since the chain was not drawn correctly. Lautrec then produced this poster, featuring the champion cyclist of the day, Constant Huret. Spoke watches in the background. A touch of lightness is added by the "bicycle-built-for-ten" in the upper left and the band. (The American Orient Cycle Company actually made a bicycle built for ten in 1896.) Huret, it would seem, is following a bicycle with at least three (triplette) or four (quadruplette) riders. Lautrec befriended the top professional cyclists of his time, including Zimmerman (*35*) and became the main supporter of the "Michaël" team of whom Bouglé was manager. Lautrec even traveled with the team to England, making sketches along the way.

Spoke's advertisements at the time emphasized maximum speed and minimum effort through the use of the Simpson chains: "Maximum de vitesse, Minimum d'effort. Cyclistes exigez la Chaine 'Levier' Simpson qui détient tous les records classiques."

This is not one of Lautrec's best posters. It simply does not have the drama, the power or the flair of his earlier works. The composition is weak; one wishes he had shown Huret alone. Again, the bicycle spokes are treated in a summary manner, although we don't have the feeling of speed. We are too distracted by the ten-man contraption going one way in the upper left and the fear that Huret is about to bump the last rider on the quadruplette in front of him. Missing here is the introspection and boldness of his more famous poster subjects, such as Jane Avril or Aristide Bruant. One would at least expect a feeling of tension in Huret's face and muscles, but he seems more relaxed than the worried rider in front of him.

29
Artist: Ferdinand Lunel. Product: Rouxel & Dubois Bicycles. Year: c. 1894. Size: 53 x 38 in. / 135 x 97 cm. Courtesy: Bibliothèque Nationale, Paris.

This is a beautifully designed poster by an artist who did few posters. That they have been able to leave the earth's gravity says much about the speed, lightness, and power of their tandem. Maindron thinks highly of Lunel and has this to say about this particular poster in his 1896 book: "This Rouxel & Dubois poster is well done; pedaling with energy, seated on a bicycle which must be perfection itself, two riders carried away by an uncommon intensity have left the earth and find themselves in the middle of the starry sky. This poster, full of distinction in its design, has a serious effect and gives the impression of a vigorous painted study."

Note the unusual design of this tandem. Tandems posed great problems, both social and technical. They were largely designed for a couple and the question was always, should the lady sit in front or in the rear? Since most tandems manufactured could only be steered from the front handlebars, it usually resolved itself in the woman providing the steering and direction from the front seat and the man providing the pedal-power behind her. However, in this Rouxel & Dubois model, both riders are not only able to pedal but to steer together as well. So that's how they made it up there! Today most tandems are built for the man up front (racing handlebars and top tube) and the back seat for the woman (depressed tube and regular handlebars).

30
Artist: Georges Gaudy (1872 - ?). Product: Legia Bicycles. Year: 1898. Size: 26 x 38 in. / 65 x 95 cm. Courtesy: Galerie Documents, Paris.

Gaudy was a Belgian painter, illustrator, and creator of numerous posters, especially on sporting themes, including many bicycle posters. In most of his posters he lays down a large area of color and emphasizes and separates his main character by means of well-defined contours, here using the color white as his border. No doubt the Japanese woodcuts, which were the rage of the day, had a great influence on him. From the standpoint of design, color or composition, this is in every way a masterful poster. The quiet, forlorn look of the sophisticated cyclist is contrasted to the almost clownish features of the riders of the odd, new threatening contraption that beckons a new era. Her expression is more that of someone looking back to simpler and more gracious days than forward to motorized travel. Again, it's a man's bicycle model which is shown, although Legia at this time also manufactured women's models.

31
Artist: Georges-Alfred Bottini (1873-1906). Product: Médinger Bicycles. Year: 1897. Size 37 x 51 in. / 93 x 129 cm. Courtesy: Bibliothèque des Arts Décoratifs, Paris.

Painter, designer and illustrator — Bottini had much in common with Toulouse-Lautrec, his contemporary, who influenced his style enormously. This poster shows the boldness, power, and realism which are the hallmark of a fine Lautrec poster. With Lautrec, Bottini was one of the few French poster artists actually from France — he was born and died in Paris — and unfortunately he met an even more premature death. And to complete the parallel, Bottini is primarily interested in setting the mood — here the emphasis on high fashion and high living — with the aid of a bicycle which, like Lautrec, he drew incorrectly. That the top bar is missing from the frame will hardly be noticed by the participants who are too busy admiring their own and their neighbors' dress — and so are we.

In April 1895, a jealous wife killed the French champion cyclist, Paul Médinger, after whom the firm was named, and then committed suicide.

32
Artist: Unknown. Product: Manège Central. Year: 1894. Size: 34 x 48 in. / 87 x 122 cm. Courtesy: Bibliothèque Nationale, Paris.

This poster, which advertises a three-rink riding school, has been attributed in every museum collection I have seen it in to Jules Chéret. Yet, although printed at his printing plant and having many of his characteristics, it is doubtful that he is the creator of this poster. Maindron, who chronicled all his posters up to 1895, and whose books were printed and proofread by Chéret, does not catalogue this work. Furthermore, all Chéret posters of this period were signed; this one is not. One is tempted to attribute this to Lucien Baylac, who worked at Chaix for a brief period, but all of Baylac's bicycle posters were printed by Kossuth rather than Chéret's Chaix firm. No matter, it's still a fine poster.

Lessons in bicycle riding were the principal purpose of these rinks, although on Sundays they also had races and it was simply fashionable to be seen there. There were restaurants and in many cases the tracks of these "Manèges" were covered for protection against rain or sun. Les-

25

26

27

28

29

30

31

32

33

sons were always more costly for the ladies; in most cases they'd be guaranteed to learn to ride a bicycle for 15 francs, whereas it would cost a man 12 francs. However, if you bought a bicycle there, lessons were thrown in free. The entrance fee was usually a half-franc, but most people bought a subscription for a month's worth of riding at 10 francs or a year's at 60 francs. It should be kept in mind that these practice rinks were especially appreciated at the time, since the tracks were kept smooth in contrast to the rough roads outside.

33
Artist: Unknown. Event: Ville du Parc Saint-Maur. Year: 1885. Size: 33 x 48 in. / 84 x 122 cm. Courtesy: Bibliothèque des Arts Décoratifs, Paris.

This poster for the large bicycle and tricycle races held at the Saint-Maur Park indicates the early popularity not only of the races themselves but of the "Ordinary" or "High-wheeler." Although a typical model might weigh as much as 60 pounds, these racing models in fact were specially built and weighed about 25 pounds each. Since a single rotation of the pedals in these non-chain bicycles caused but a single rotation of the front wheel, the larger the diameter the faster the bicycle. Some of these went to about 60 inches (152 cm) and thus placed a premium on long legs.

By the year this poster was made, competition for the manufacture of these first true bicycles was fierce and many racers were subsidized by their manufacturers. In England alone there were two hundred firms making Ordinaries (sometimes called "penny farthings") in 1885 and over 400,000 cyclists. Tremendous speeds could be attained, some going over 20 miles an hour, quite remarkable in view of solid tires and rough roads.

In all these races, strict rules were observed and usually classified as to amateur and professional, and divided by type of bicycle. As can be seen here, the prizes, ranging from medals to 50 francs, were not themselves the attraction; most riders were paid by manufacturers anxious to show-off their wares. A year earlier, in 1884, Thomas Stevens became the first man to cross the United States by riding such an "Ordinary" — A fifty-inch diameter on a 75 pound machine — from Oakland, California, to Boston, Massachusetts, in 103 days. From a point of view of design, the well-delineated forms and expressions of the three riders makes this otherwise "busy" black-and-white poster most interesting. There is an almost woodcut treatment to this lithograph.

34
Artist: Unknown. Product: Cyclone Bicycles. Year: c. 1885. Size: 39 x 55 in. / 100 x 139 cm. Courtesy: Bibliothèque des Arts Décoratifs, Paris.

This poster for a bicycle "without chains" gives the name and address of both store and factory, and shows some of the refinements of the "Ordinary." The difference between front and back wheel is decreasing, the seat has been "cushioned" by a steel spring action, and most important is the "double pignon," a variation of the gear differential which was around the corner.

This color lithograph is singular for the proud bearing and high fashion of the rider; his suit is blue and the type is predominantly yellow. In some versions, there is an additional few inches at the bottom with the type "Représenté par:" after which could be added the name and address of the local agent selling the Cyclone in the provinces.

35
Artist: George Moore. Product: Raleigh Bicycles. Year: 1893. Size: 41 x 59 in. / 105 x 150 cm. Courtesy: Bibliothèque Nationale, Paris.

Arthur-Auguste Zimmerman of New York was one of the most successful and colorful cyclists of his time, competing for prizes and much attention in the United States and throughout Europe. He befriended several artists, including Toulouse-Lautrec, and his conviviality and unorthodox training methods — he often smoked cigars while chatting with friends for most of the night before a big race — endeared him to the public at large. He was only 22 when this poster was published but was already world-renowned. "Zimmie" made the Raleigh road racer of 1892, shown here, quite famous with his winning sprints. He won over 1,400 races and, on arriving in England in 1892, he won the British National Championships at one, five and fifty mile distances, and established world records at the half and quarter mile sprints before returning to the United States. In 1895, an American newspaper, decrying the overcommercialization and multiplicity of races, recalled "the old days" when "there were comparatively few racing men. To be a Zimmerman was to be a better-known man than the president of the United States."

There were several versions of this poster, with differing banners below the line "Champion of the World." The one shown here is for the Paris agent of Raleigh, who, with almost all other such agencies, moved to the Avenue de la Grande Armée shortly after this poster was published. The Raleigh was advertised throughout France as "La Meilleure Bicyclette du Monde" (The World's Finest Bicycle). In another version of this poster, the bottom banner proclaims: "Having upon the Raleigh, Defeated all Comers in the United States, England, Scotland, Ireland, France, Germany and Canada" and gives Raleigh's factory and head office address for England (in Nottingham) and for the United States (on Bank and Greenwich Streets, New York City).

George Moore was also an English export, calling the "Nouvelle Athènes" café on Place Pigalle the real training grounds for his art and inspiration. He did several bicycle posters, including some for J. K. Starley's Rover, as well as the Matador Cycles poster (*73*).

36
Artist: Frank Chesworth. Event: Surrey Bicycle Club. Year: 1895. Size: 20 x 30 in. / 51 x 76 cm. Courtesy: Bibliothèque Nationale, Paris.

If this book included posters for bicycle publications, one would have preferred Chesworth's poster for the weekly "King of the Road" magazine. But this two-color lithograph does show the style and flair which made him, along with Dudley Hardy, John Hassall and Aubrey Beardsley, one of the finest English poster artists of the turn of the century.

Bicycle clubs abounded — there were over 300 in England at the time of this Meeting — and the Surrey was one of the oldest and most exclusive ones. Certainly Chesworth makes it clear that this is the one which attracts the "smart set" of London, although it is typical of English posterists to make their women highly aristocratic. The Club conducted outings, team matches with other clubs, races at which large prizes were offered and, in 1880, always on the lookout for new challenges, it created a hill-climbing competition. The meeting at Kennington Oval is advertised as coming under the rules of the N.C.U. The National Cycling Union represented the interests of the clubs, and of cyclists generally.

37
Artist: W. S. Rogers. Event: Stanley Show of Cycles. Year: 1899. Size: 19 x 30 in. / 49 x 76 cm. Courtesy: Bibliothèque des Arts Décoratifs, Paris.

The Bicycle Show was an institution in England before it became a popular yearly event in France in 1894 (see Forain's poster, page 20). The Stanley Show, begun in 1878, was especially important, since it introduced new models each year, and many bicycles made their world debut here. The first chain-driven Safety bicycle was exhibited at the Stanley Show of 1880 by Tangent Bicycle Company (which became Rudge); the first "Rover" safety appeared in 1884; and the 1892 Stanley Show introduced such new brands as Gladiator, Clément, Rouxel et Dubois, Peugeot et Megret, Vincent & Cie., and Michelin, among others. Until their own Salon became well-established, Frenchmen in large numbers traveled across the Channel each year to see the newest wonders on wheels. One of those wonders in 1899 was the upcoming "motor carriage."

This four-color lithographic poster by Rogers is quite charming and, from the point of design and composition is almost perfect. Rogers was not only a posterist, but a writer and theoretician of the medium.

38
Artist: O'Galop. Product: Michelin Tires. Year: 1896. Size: 47 x 63 in. / 121 x 160 cm. Courtesy: Galerie Documents, Paris.

This poster marks the beginning of the "Bibendum" symbol of Michelin, France's leading manufacturer of tires. O'Galop, principally a cartoonist, developed this series which became the company's trademark over the years. The Latin phrase at top means "Now we can drink" and below it, "To your health." The bottom headline makes the picture perfectly clear: "The Michelin tire drinks all obstacles." Here Michelin, or Bibendum, is seen fearlessly taking on — or taking in — broken glass and other "obstacles" without trepidation. The cigar, no doubt, adds to the feeling of confidence, although that assurance is not shared by brand X and Y on either side.

Although an air tire using rubber and leather had been invented in 1845, it was not until John Boyd Dunlop, a Belfast veterinary surgeon, experimented with air-filled pneumatic tires for bicycles that this invention revolutionized the bicycle industry beginning in 1888, adding speed and comfort to the new "safety" bicycles of the 1890's by replacing solid tires used until then. Competition was as fierce among tire manufacturers as it had been all along with bicycle brands.

André and Edouard Michelin received their patent, for pneumatic tires with beaded edges secured on the wheel rims by rings, in 1892. Dunlop's detachable wired on type had been bought by his company from another inventor, Charles Welch. A good deal of litigation developed over who had the right to what kind of tire, but in 1897 Dunlop finally lost its suit against Michelin.

39
Artist: E. Montaut. Product: Roussel Wheels. Year: 1897. Size: 39 x 55 in. / 100 x 138 cm. Courtesy: Bibliothèque des Arts Décoratifs, Paris.

Although Michelin soon established itself as the leading manufacturer of bicycle tires, and much later of automobile tires as well, its fat, air-filled pneumatic tires had to withstand much abuse at first, as can be seen in this highy anti-Michelin poster. At the top: "The Tire . . . is enslavement!" and at the bottom, "The elastic Roussel wheel is Freedom!!" Its one competitive edge was that it could not blow out, but, of course, Michelin had the last laugh and it, rather than the solid Roussel wheel, became the standard of tire excellence. This poster caused further litigation and Michelin was successful in preventing its further distribution.

40
Artist: Unknown. Product: Humber Bicycles. Year: c. 1895. Size: 22 x 30 in. / 56 x 76 cm. Courtesy: Batavus Museum, Heerenveen, Holland.

With competition beginning to stiffen in the late 1890's and overproduction saturating the market, companies went bankrupt and others merged. Three who successfully merged in 1896 were Clément, Gladiator and Humber. And eventually in 1932 the cycle interests of Humber Limited were acquired by Raleigh Industries, the world's largest manufacturer of bicycles. The Humber brand is still being sold by Raleigh today.

Humber produced many more posters for its Paris agency at 18 Rue du 4 Septembre than for its main London showroom at Holborn Viaduct. All its French advertisements and posters proclaimed the Humber as "Première Marque du Monde." (The World's Finest Make.)

This poster, as so many others at the time, clearly shows the emancipating influence that the bicycle had on women. And as with almost all posters in which men and women are depicted, it's the woman who does the leading and, in this case it would seem the beckoning as well. Maybe she just wants to show them her new Humber.

41
Artist: Unknown. Product: Crawford Bicycles. Year: c. 1895. Size: 20 x 30 in. / 52 x 76 cm. Courtesy: Bibliothèque Nationale, Paris.

As with most American companies in the 1890's, export was a large part of the business, and the

34
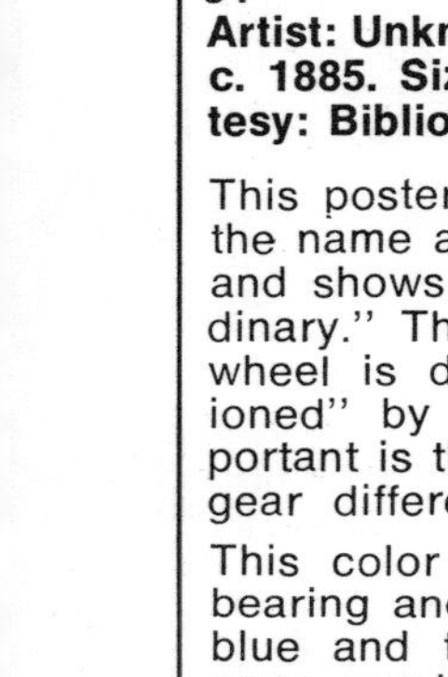

35
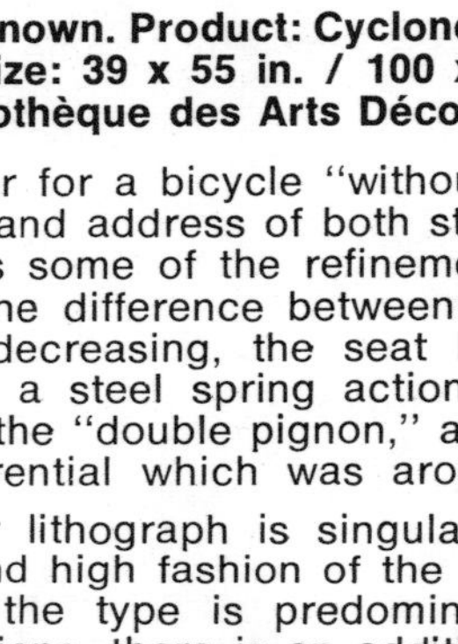

36

37
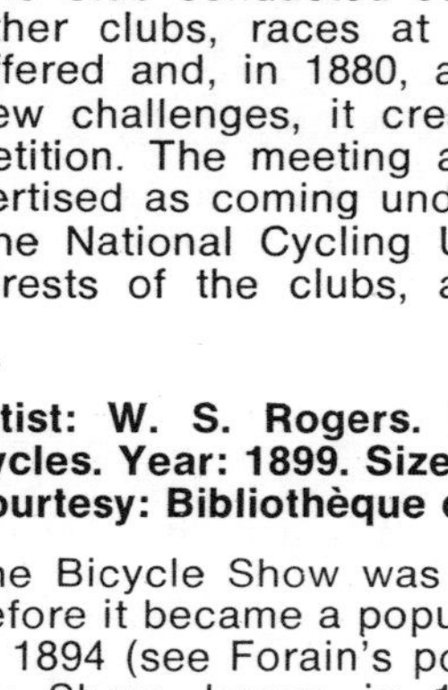

38
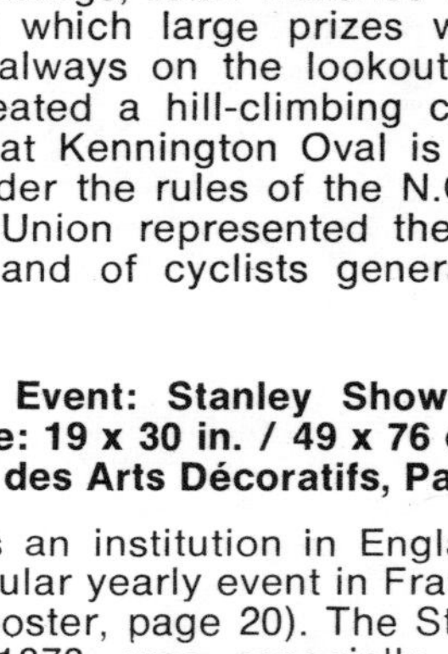

39
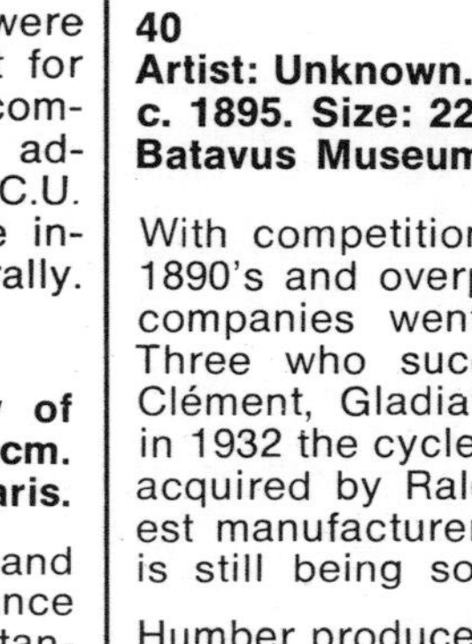

40
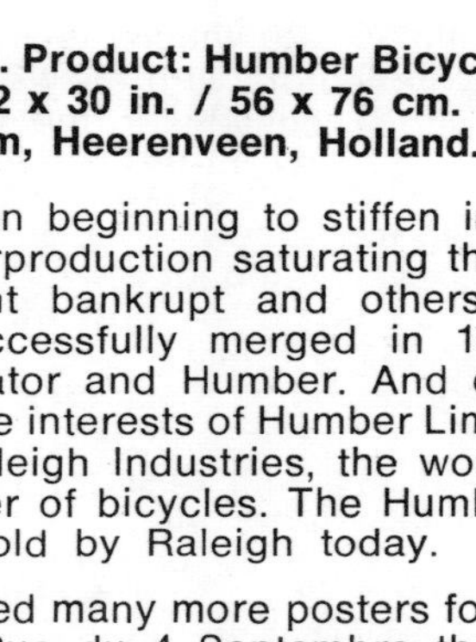

41

same design appeared in several countries. For their French agency, the address, 22 Avenue de la Grande Armée, was added to the bottom. This artist too — whoever he may be — could not cope with spokes, although here it adds not so much to the feeling of speed as to one of lightness as the pretty lady seems to be floating over the road — or is it over the globe?

42
Artist: L.W. Product: Gladiator Bicycles. Year: c. 1895. Size: 55 x 39 in. / 140 x 100 cm. Courtesy: Athena Reproductions, London.

There is an almost surrealistic quality about this sensuous design for Gladiator. In this large four-color lithograph the flowing hair is golden, the background blue and the type and bicycle green. The tips of the wings on the pedals are a flaming orange-red. I know nothing of the artist, whose initials are "L.W.," other than the fact that he knew how to sell bicycles.

As previously indicated, there was a financial merger of three leading companies in 1896: Gladiator, Clément and Humber. But each kept its own identity and brand name. And if Pal is the artist who created more bicycle posters than any other artist, then there is probably a close race between Gladiator and Clement as to which company commissioned and executed more posters than any other. I have found at least one hundred examples of each.

At this time, all the Gladiator advertisements had one of two headlines: "Les Plus Beaux Records du Monde" (the world's best records) to be followed by such information as "1000 kil. en 24 heures 12 m., 100 kil. en 2 heures 0 m. 35 s." (That's about 621 miles covered in 24 hours and 12 minutes and 62 miles in two hours.) The other and more frequently seen headline would simply and modestly proclaim "Sans Egale est la Bicyclette Gladiator." (The Gladiator Bicycle is without equal.)

43
Artist: Paolo Henri. Product: Gladiator Bicycles. Year: c. 1900. Size: 54 x 33 in. / 136 x 84 cm. Courtesy: Batavus Museum, Heerenveen, Holland

So where's the bicycle? A question that can be asked of many bicycle posters. When Gladiator said "Sans Egale" (see above), it might also have meant that it was in a social class all its own. For if the first poster proves that sex sells, then this one proves that snob appeal can also move the product. The latest fashions are shown in this two-color lithograph which depicts the social élite of Paris.

There were many "rip-offs" in the poster business at the turn of the century — as there are today. A "rip-off" is a modification of larceny, since the product is not stolen but only slightly modified. At that time it was the practice to slightly change the design of a poster so that when a new bicycle model was introduced or a poster size had to be changed you would not have to pay the artist again. (A new size or design required new lithographic stones, since these were not photo-offset, and it was simpler and cheaper to have one of the engravers in the printing shop copy an earlier poster design.) There are several versions of this Henri original; one, much smaller (26 x 14 in. / 67 x 37 cm), in green and black, has altered the dress and facial expressions of the characters slightly (the men with top hats to the left and right of the center girls have grown about six inches, so that Henri's original design which most prominently played up the girl in the middle and gave it some form is now marred) and also omitted the artist's name. They did remember to leave in the trademark of Gladiator: The jockey-on-horse-on-globe.

44
Artist: Unknown. Product: Bingham Bicycles. Year: c. 1892. Size: 30 x 39 in. / 76 x 104 cm. Courtesy: Bibliothèque Nationale, Paris.

I can say little about this poster, largely due to ignorance of the work and partly due to the "stunning" effect of it. The poster was printed in Man-chester, England, for the Dutch agent, "Twees-paak" whose Rotterdam address appears on the first line of copy. The winged-figure with medals makes a truly imposing figure.

45
Artist: Unknown. Product: Dürkopp Bicycles. Year: c. 1900. Size: 24 x 35 in. / 60 x 89 cm. Courtesy: Staatsgalerie Baden - Württemberg, Stuttgart.

This beautifully designed poster was produced by the well-known Viennese lithographer, J. Weiner. Although lithographers themselves frequently provided the design, this is not the case here, so the artist remains unknown. It was unfortunately typical of German-Austrian poster lithographers of the time to print only the credit line for the printing firm and not the name of the individual who actually designed the art for it. This may do wonders for a company's *esprit* but it's maddening to collectors. The background is a tone of blue and all the art and lettering is black.

Dürrkopp A.G. Bielefeld was founded in 1898, becoming Bielefelder Maschinenfabrik in 1913 and continuing bicycle production until shortly after World War II. A later and totally different treatment for the same company's product can be seen on page 72.

46
Artist: E. Célos. Product: Brantford Canadian Bicycles. Year: 1901. Sizes 36 x 49 in. / 92 x 124 cm. Courtesy: Batavus Museum, Heerenveen, Holland.

A striking example of Art Nouveau style by an artist obviously influenced by Privat-Livemont and Mucha and their eastern exoticism. But it does not carry ornamentation to the ridiculous; it is well designed and the hint of the bicycle in the cut-out wheel works is well integrated in the composition, making the wheel almost another flower at first glance. Here again, it was elegance, femininity and social self-assurance which was being sold. If that came across, then the bicycles would find their customers.

The Canada Cycle & Motor Company was formed by an amalgamation of ten Canadian bicycle manufacturers at the turn of the century, one of the brands being the Brantford. The company, known as C.C.M., was subsequently taken over by Seaway Multicorp Ltd. of Weston, Ontario, of which it is now a division and the only manufacturer of bicycles in Canada.

47
Artist: Unknown. Product: Humber's Danish Bicycles. Year: c. 1900. Size: 24 x 34 in. / 62 x 86 cm. Courtesy: Bibliothèque Nationale, Paris.

This poster was printed by the Danish lithographer, Frode Hass, for Humber's Copenhagen subsidiary. It is not clear if Hass was simply the lithographer or also the designer of the poster. At any rate, the design is excellent and the characters quite amusing. Again it's the woman in the lead, and although Humber pioneered lightweight bicycles, they still required spokes to hold the frame and wheels together and there is not a hint of them here.

48
Artist: PAL (pseudonym for Jean de Paléologue, born 1855). Product: Liberator Bicycles. Year: c. 1900. Size: 39 x 57 in. / 105 x 144 cm. Courtesy: Batavus Museum, Heerenveen, Holland.

This is the second of three Pal posters in this collection (see also pages 25 and 62), and as previously noted, he was a prolific poster artist who frequently used classical figures in his work. In this four-color lithograph Pal depicts a proud "Soldat Gaulois" who is either protecting others with the help of her Liberator Cycle or is standing guard over this most valuable vehicle. One has the feeling that Pal enjoyed his work — and his women.

49
Artist: C. M. Coolidge. Product: Columbia Bicycles. Year: c. 1895. Size: 20 x 25 in. / 51 x 64 cm. Courtesy: Library of Congress, Washington.

Little is known of this poster or this artist, but if ever there was a poster that needed little explanation, it's this one.

Albert A. Pope had first seen the modern bicycle — a British high-wheel "ordinary" — at the Centennial Exhibition in Philadelphia in 1876. He became enthused over its possibilities and went to England to survey the market. He started to import British bikes the next year and began to manufacture his own "Columbia" ordinary in 1878. Thus began the American bicycle industry.

Pope was a master salesman and promoter and did much to popularize bicycles in the United States through publicity and advertising, especially with many colorful posters, and by underwriting the publication of bicycle magazines. He was also a merchandising genius and set up hundreds of distributorships across the United States to sell the Columbia at a fixed price. It is in these showrooms that this poster was hung. He founded a riding school and one of the first bicycle clubs and he championed the building of better and smoother roads. But these high-wheelers, over 70 pounds in weight, many costing more than $300.00 (the average factory worker earned about $30.00 a month at the time), had a limited market and it was not until about 1890, with the introduction of the chain-driven safety bicycle that cycling became the craze of America. At first the tubular steel was imported from England, but by 1896 American factories began producing their own steel tubing. A combination of rising market demand and overproduction forced prices down and the bicycle came within the reach of the working man. In 1895, the approximate year of publication of this poster, about 800,000 bicycles were manufactured in the United States, increasing to 2 million in 1897. Prices dropped to about $100.00 each, and in some cases even far below this sum. Part of this overproduction was sent overseas and advertisements throughout France proclaimed the Columbia "Les Meilleurs du Monde" and Columbia set up shop there, first at Rue de Choiseul and then, like all the other bicycle firms on Avenue de la Grande-Armée.

Although the typeface used here is restrained and typical of American posters of the period, the advertisements were hard-sell. Announced an 1894 advertisement: "The mental rest and exhilaration that comes through the gentle exercise of riding a wheel — the sense of life and freedom that only a wheelman knows — that can be yours if you will. Go thou and buy a bicycle; to learn is easy. Get a Columbia." Some of the best artists of the day, such as Penfield, Parrish and Bradley were kept busy turning out yearly catalogues for the new cycles. Columbia Bicycles are produced today by the Columbia Manufacturing Company of Westfield, Massachusetts, a subsidiary of MTD Products, Inc.

50
Artist: John Hassall (1868-1948) Product: Beeston Tires. Year: 1896. Size: 30 x 20 in. / 76 x 50 cm. Courtesy: Bibliothèque des Arts Décoratifs, Paris.

Along with his friend Dudley Hardy, John Hassall was one of the most popular artists of his day — and one of the most prolific. He illustrated many books, especially children's books, and his work appeared in many journals. But he is best known for more than 600 posters he created. He studied the classical art methods in both Belgium and France, but did almost all his work in England, personally making the lithographic stones for all his posters at David Allen and Sons. He became the "Poster King" of England and is best known for his many theatrical posters. Hassall said that the three things a poster artist needed most were "ideas, ideas, ideas!" His way of executing them was a light caricature style which endeared itself to a large appreciative public — and this, after all, is the most important need of a poster. An excellent appreciation of his work appears in Bevis Hillier's book, "Posters."

The Beeston tires, which "Go by themselves", were part of the Humber enterprises and Hassall's "idea" here is apparently to convey the impression that they are so good that they don't even need a bicycle to get going.

51
Artist: Will H. Bradley (1868-1962) Product: Victor Bicycles. Year: 1896. Size: 40 x 28 in. / 102 x 71 cm. Courtesy: The SandyVal Graphics Ltd. Collection.

Another Bradley poster for Victor has been previously noted (24). Here spokes might have marred the composition of the poster and their absence gives a feeling of lightness and airiness to the bicycle and the entire design. The gentleman to the left, we may assume, is also on a bicycle, but it's not clear if he's eying her or her Victor. A third Bradley design is on page 57.

52
Artist: Jules Chéret (1836-1933). Product: L'Etendard Français Bicycles. Year: 1891. Size: 33 x 46 in. / 83 x 117 cm. Courtesy: Victoria & Albert Museum, London.

Chéret is the founder of the colored pictorial poster and probably its most prolific and influential practitioner. By 1895, the critic Ernest Maindron had carefully catalogued over 800 posters by Chéret. By 1900, when he did his last poster, estimates vary as to whether he had produced over 1,200 or over 1,300 posters. But the quantity, although quite impressive, is not as important as the quality of his work or the incalculable contribution he made to color lithography and especially its application to poster art. It was Chéret who showed France, and the world, that it was possible to artistically and economically produce large color posters. His use of overlapping color stones to achieve bright colors of limitless shades and tones is still remarkable when viewed today. Although he did abandon ink in favor of the lithographic crayon to achieve increased subtlety, this was not done at so much of a cost in sharp color contrasts as this reproduction might indicate. This poster, from the collection of the Victoria & Albert Museum, probably had much brighter, more vivid reds and blues than can be shown here; this fading is less due to time than to the incredible negligence on the part of the Victoria & Albert, which keeps its posters (and it has about 80 by Chéret) folded, most without linen backing, with ink pressed against ink. Many are simply crumbling and cracking. And this in the Museum which provided Chéret with much inspiration while he learned the lithographic trade in London! (Why? Museum officials claim they lack the space to keep posters individually rolled in tubes or properly hung and linen-backed; folded sheets take less space. I suppose if things get really cramped they'd melt the Crown Jewels!)

As with all of Chéret's posters, it's more a "joie de vivre" than a specific product which is being sold, and the means of selling is always a gay, vivacious, pretty girl which became his trademark. "Les Chérettes," as they became known, were all over his posters and all over the walls of Paris, and the one shown here is quite typical. He is best known for his posters advertising the Folies-Bergère, the Palais de Glace, Dubonnet and Saxoleine. He won the admiration of all Frenchmen and the praise of almost all critics; his wide popularity, in evidence on the walls of Paris, was affirmed when he received the decoration of the Légion d'Honneur in 1890, the year before this poster was executed.

Surprisingly enough, although his printing firm, Chaix, which was next door to the large Clément Bicycle Company, produced many bicycle posters, Chéret himself designed few of them. He did a colorful one for Cleveland bicycles, in which the Chérette happily waves an American flag, as well as an earlier one for the Paris-Course-Hippodrome.

This poster for the Bicycle Workshop at the Quai d'Orsay advertises the French Banner and makes a pitch for the ride-now-pay-later plan: 50 francs

on delivery and 25 francs per month thereafter. For this we are assured of getting the latest model, elegant and well-built, but are not told how many months we must go on paying.

After 1900, Chéret gave up posters and concentrated on other art forms, including oil and pastel paintings and tapestry designs. He began to lose his sight and became blind shortly before World War I. Fittingly (or ominously) enough, his last poster, about 1900, was for an automobile fuel, "Benzo-Moteur."

53
Artist: Decam. Product: Caténol Bicycles. Year: 1897. Size: 31 x 63 in. / 80 x 159 cm. Courtesy: Bibliothèque des Arts Décoratifs, Paris.

W. S. Rogers as previously noted, indicated that one of the subtle qualities which a poster should have is that of "reticence," leaving something for the imagination of the spectator to supply. "The public likes a problem picture, and is ever ready to exercise its ingenuity in providing the missing link in the story." There are obviously many links in this story, which is actually an advertising poster for a bicycle. The headline, "La Vérité Assise!!!" can be literally translated as "The Truth is Seated" or more figuratively as "The Truth is Established." There is an old French proverb which says "La Verité sort du puits," — the truth comes out of wells. Or, if you dig down deep enough, you'll get at the bottom of things. How all this relates to the young lady, the chains, the "evil eye" she casts, the bicycle chain-gear-pedal which forms the waterwell mechanism — all this I leave to the reader's "imagination" and "ingenuity." Vive la vérité!

54
Artist: Unknown. Event: Vélodrome Buffalo. Year: c. 1894. Size: 47 x 33 in. / 120 x 83 cm. Courtesy: Bibliothèque Nationale, Paris.

If the year 1872-73 marked the start of the modern bicycle era, then the year 1891 marked, in many ways, the beginning of its real popularity. Races were organized, the safety bicycle was coming into its own, detachable pneumatic tires made riding more comfortable, and the bicycle was no longer a toy of the leisurely few but a vehicle of fun, sport and transportation for the working man. And the year 1891 also saw the opening of that peculiarly Parisian institution, the Vélodrome. It was a great outdoor theatre, with tracks for competition, rinks for learners, a place where one could dine and be entertained, where one could buy, rent or repair his bicycle, and the big crowds came out on Sunday for the biggest attraction of all, the races. ("Courses tous les Dimanches" announces the poster.)

But the vélodrome was obviously a social as well as athletic institution. Wrote Maindron in 1896: "The vélodromes are now more and more attended; ladies come in large numbers and falls are frequent: one doesn't get bored in these establishments. In any case, we are a happy people, even having had once an 'Echassodrome.' " (A track where men on stilts would race against one another.)

Of the four vélodromes which opened at that time — le Parc des Princes, le Vélodrome d'Hiver, the summer one of Vincennes, and the Buffalo, it was the latter which was the most popular. As was noted earlier (28), Tristan Bernard was the director of the Buffalo and his friend Toulouse-Lautrec was a frequent spectator. It derived its name from the fact that Colonel W. F. Cody's very popular Buffalo Bill circus had been staged on that spot, which became known as the Buffalo Grounds, and subsequently when the Vélodrome was built there, it was called the Buffalo Vélodrome. Even when the Vélodrome Buffalo moved to the Porte d'Orleans, it still retained the name of its former circus spot.

Although the lithographer of this poster is F. Appel, it is not clear if in this case he also designed it.

55
Artist: Alphonse Mucha (1860-1939) Product: Waverley Cycles. Year: 1898. Size: 45 x 35 in. / 115 x 90 cm. Courtesy: Bibliothèque Nationale, Paris.

The Czech artist Mucha became an overnight sensation with his quickly executed Sarah Bernhardt poster at Christmas-time 1894, while he was at the Lemercier printing firm in Paris. The famed actress needed a poster immediately and all the other artists were out of town during the holiday season. Mucha volunteered; the rest is history. For the next five years he did all of Sarah Bernhardt's posters and after her quarrel with Lemercier he went under contract to Champenois, the printer of this and all subsequent Mucha posters.

Mucha has become synonymous with Art Nouveau. But there is more than the flower, the women, the flowing hair, and the mysticism associated with this style in Mucha's work. There is also a very strong, sure sense of composition that never allows him to slip into banality and confusion; no matter how much décor, the central character, theme or product is always clearly and boldly delineated. His contrasting use of strong and muted colors added to the glow and richness of his work. And all his finest traits are realized in this masterful poster for Waverley.

W. S. Rogers, the British poster artist and historian whom I have quoted earlier, said of this work: "The advertiser, who exceptionally only is an expert in these matters (of poster design), if he is, say, a cycle manufacturer, will insist on his machine being correctly drawn to the smallest details, forgetting that the seething, hurrying crowd has not time to take in and appreciate these minutiae. Such an advertiser should study the beautiful design by the French artist, Mucha, for Waverley Cycles, in which the handle-bar and front pillar only appear in the picture. The artist, however, has drawn, an attractive female figure holding a branch of bay to typify 'ascendency,' whilst she rests her arm upon an anvil, on which is a hammer, suggestive of the mechanical nature of the industry. A poster of this character lingers in the memory when others less simple in their appeal are forgotten."

Mucha designed this poster for Harry Reynaud, the French importer of the American bicycle, Waverley. Advertisements for Waverley Cycles in France at this time proclaimed it the "Grande Marque Américaine."

56
Artist: Henri Thiriet. Product: Omega Bicycles. Year: c. 1895. Size: 36 x 55 in. / 99 x 140 cm. Courtesy: Bibliothèque des Arts Décoratifs, Paris.

This is yet another example of the Art Nouveau poster at its stylized best. The composition has been meticulously — almost geometrically — arranged, and the influence of mythology, in both the Greek name for the bicycle brand of Kreutzberger and the winged goddess, plus the bold use of flat and vibrant colors emphasize this.

Unlike the previous Thiriet poster (27), we get to see a bit more of the bicycle, and it turns out that the Omega is chainless ("Sans Chaine"), even though continuous-chain-driven bicycles were being produced at this time. It worked by means of bevel gears.

57
Artist: Will H. Bradley (1868-1962). Event: Springfield Bicycle Club Tournament. Year: 1895. Size: 14 x 21 in. / 36 x 53 cm. Courtesy: Library of Congress, Washington.

This is the third of three Bradley posters shown in this book (see also 24 and 51). And a look at all three shows the strength and also the diversity of style of which this talented artist was capable. He could be full of flowery ornament (as with the first Victor bicycle poster) or he could be very bold and striking in a more modern style, as shown here. And he could change paces when advertising the same event: The next Springfield Club Tournament poster he designed was completely bordered with flowers.

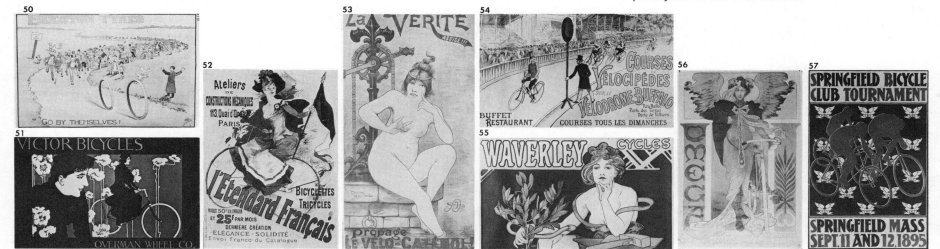

Although the Stanley Show in England (see *37*) was the first Bicycle Show ever held, the first one in the United States was held in Springfield, Massachusetts, in 1883, and this city became a center of cycling enthusiasm for the entire country. And the enthusiasm was especially great for cycle races, such as those sponsored by the Springfield Club. They were held on a smooth track prepared for maximum sprint speeds, with a circumference of about a third of a mile. Bradley had just moved to Springfield in 1895 to set up his Wayside Press.

It is hard for us today to imagine how completely captivated Americans were by the bicycle and especially by such events as this Club Tournament. Here was America at the height of its bicycle craze. Thousands turned out. The first day was devoted to qualifying heats and social events, such as balls and meetings of the League of American Wheelmen (L.A.W.). Entertainment abounded: Professor Lewis ascended a huge balloon which advertised Stearns bicycle products; the second regiment band played for the spectators. The *Springfield Daily Republican* reported that "in the evening bicycle gossip was all that could be heard anywhere. Bicyclists owned the town . . . and considerable betting was seen . . . An immense crowd was congregated there all the evening and traffic on the street was completely congested. Unless one was of athletic build it was a matter of some difficulty to get to the Springfield bicycle club rooms . . . Young women were strongly in evidence, and so was the 'chaffing' between them and the frolicksome young bicylists, who, for the time being, are something of demi-gods . . . The band played all the evening, and the crowd filled the park and overflowed into most of the neighboring streets. . . . On the third floor (of the L.A.W. headquarters) there was an informal 'smoker' and all the means for affording the devotee of the weed delight, from a cob pipe to cigarettes, were there in abundance." In the major event of dozens of races, the fastest competition mile on record was broken when W. C. Sanger went the distance in 2.01-3/5 minutes in the International Professional Mile.

58
Artist: René Péan. Product: Châlet du Cycle. Year: 1899. Size: 35 x 49 in. / 88 x 125 cm. Courtesy: Bibliothèque Nationale, Paris.

Properly speaking, this poster does not fall within the scope of this book, but I have included it because it does give a very good feel and flavor of the times and the importance of the bicycle. There were many such "Châlets" all around Paris which at this time was still almost completely surrounded by woods and forests, this one being the Châlet in the Woods of Boulogne. These cafes were meeting places for all Parisian cyclists. The social importance of the bicycle is well shown in this poster, although it can also be seen that the motorcycle and the automobile were beginning to threaten the quiet of the landscape.

René Péan was a student of Chéret and worked in Chéret's printing plant, Chaix, where this poster was produced, before going on to a career in stage design.

59
Artist: N. Vivien. Product: Hirondelle-St. Etienne Bicycles. Year: c. 1900. Size: 43 x 53 in. / 108 x 135 cm. Courtesy: Batavus Museum, Heerenveen, Holland.

This is a fascinating bicycle poster — yes, a bicycle poster. "Hirondelle" means swallows and this brand name is appropriate enough since the swallow is a bird known for its speed, grace and dependability (or regular migrations) and these are qualities the bicycle manufacturer wishes to emulate and convey to the public. Do the birds, as shown here, also represent a new-found freedom and the Gothic structure from which they alight the old and restricted life of the pre-bicycle era? Such deep meaning or symbolic treatment I leave to the reader, but it really doesn't matter. The sheer beauty of the poster is so captivating that we'll surely remember "Hirondelle" when we're buying our next bicycle. But don't ask for it by name: Hirondelle is gone, but its parent company, St. Etienne, is still in business, making arms. Now how does *that* grab you as a fit subject for your daily deep-think exercise?

My ignorance of the artist, whose signature seems to be "N. Vivien" is total. To the right of it is the mark of the lithographer, Gallice.

60
Artist: Unknown. Product: Michelin Tires. Year: c. 1905. Size: 42 x 56 in. / 107 x 143 cm. Courtesy: Batavus Museum, Heerenveen, Holland.

Another beautiful and allegorical representation to tell us that Michelin is the wave (or the wheel) of the future. The bottom line announces that it is the only brand which adapts itself to the wheel of fortune. In spite of the positive attributes of this wave, it is the forlorn and wistful look of the little girl, left behind with her broken old non-Michelin tire, that is the visual point of interest. Honest. The artist is unknown, although an "M" underlined and inside a circle, does appear on the lower right hand corner. The printer is Brunoff of Paris.

61
Artist: Unknown. Product: March-Davis Bicycles. Year: 1897. Size: 40 x 84 in. / 102 x 213 cm. Courtesy: Library of Congress, Washington.

This is further evidence that the overproduction of American bicycles was not only leading to bankruptcies of smaller firms and heavy emphasis on exports, but also to trade wars, in which manufacturers and retail outlets competed for the lowest prices to attract customers and deplete their inventory. The winner was the consumer and the bicycle was within reach of the working man. In this almost photographic treatment, the artist has given us every detail, spokes and all. The Strobridge Company of Cincinnati was America's leading printer of posters at the turn of the century.

62
Artist: PAL (pseudonym for Jean de Paléologue, born 1855). Product: Déesse Bicycles. Year: c. 1898. Size: 41 x 56 in. / 104 x 142 cm. Courtesy: Galerie Documents, Paris.

This is the third bicycle poster by Pal presented in this volume (see also pages 25 and 48) and, as indicated, he was a prolific posterist, especially in the field of cycle art. And as noted also, he used popular classical figures of the times, such as goddesses, in his posters. Here the bicycle manufacturer himself has stolen this motif, making the brand name of his cycle "Déesse" which means Goddess. Also being sold here is a Skidproof ("Antiderapant") Kosmos brand tire (see letters on front wheel). Deitz is probably the French agent of the Kosmos brand and the licensee of Dunlop (see Kosmos poster, page 80). "Déesse" was the French brand name of the Rudge Bicycle Company, which subsequently merged with Whitworth and in 1943 was acquired by Raleigh.

This is an excellent design, combining the boldness of the central figure with the interest of the crowds below without in any way making it seem "busy"; the composition is quite deliberate and good. It claims your immediate attention and then draws you nearer, involving you in the details of the work. Pal loved to portray well-endowed, semi-clad women, with bare breasts almost always prominently on view. But this poster was considered especially erotic at the time for one did not so sensuously and explicitly reveal madame's "derrière" as he does here. One would be tempted to call Pal "a dirty old man" if it did not reveal some possible like traits in those who much admire and collect his work. Note also that, as befits a "goddess," she rules not only over the Paris skyline, but over the entire globe, as evidenced by the diverse national and ethnic make-up of the awe-struck citizens below.

63
Artist: Misti (pseudonym for Ferdinand Misti-Mifliez). Product: Clément Bicycles. Year: c. 1900. Size: 17 x 25 in. / 45 x 65 cm. Courtesy: Private Collection.

As previously noted, the two firms which accounted for more posters than any other were Clément and Gladiator, and Misti designed posters for both of them, as well as for Rouxel et Dubois, for the Vélodrome d'Hiver and an excellent one for the cycle magazine, *Le Vélo.* This small poster was meant for in-store use by Clément. The rooster, seen here in background on a bicycle wheel, is the symbol of France. Misti, who at his best combines some of the lightness of Chéret and the bold strokes and outlines of Cappiello, was a lithographer in Chéret's Chaix printing works, although most of the posters he himself designed were printed by other firms such as Bataille, Appel and, in this case, Bourgerie. He was an industrial designer and also contributed art work for several journals, although he is most closely associated with *L'Assiette au Beurre.*

64
Artist: Brynolf Wennerberg (1866-1950). Product: Cless & Plessing Bicycles. Year: c. 1898. Size: 33 x 46 in. / 83 x 117 cm. Courtesy: Berghaus Verlag.

Wennerberg was a Swedish artist who worked mainly in Munich, both as painter and lithographer, as well as illustrator for *Simplizissimus.* The Austrian bicycle firm of Cless & Plessing were, according to this poster, "Specialists in Chainless Bicycles." And although the man with the broken chain has obviously got a problem, it was, even by this time the chain-driven bicycle which was the wave of the future. This fine six-color lithograph was produced by one of the best printers of the day, Grimme & Hempel of Leipzig, whose other posters in this book can be seen on pages 67, 70 and 71.

65
Artist: Unknown. Product: Clément Bicycles. Year: c. 1900. Size: 36 x 53 in. / 97 x 135 cm. Courtesy: Batavus Museum, Heerenveen, Holland.

This poster is reproduced in the beautiful book *Paris, 1900,* in which Hermann Schardt attributes it to Misti and provides a date of 1903. Neither of these facts appear on the face of the poster and although I would be willing to accept the date, I find it difficult to accept the attribution, for it would be most untypical of Misti to design such a poster. His style (as can only slightly be gleaned from the previous Clément poster, page 63), is just not this lyrical nor this deliberately decorative; it is more explicit and direct. Nor is this face one which can be seen in any other Misti poster. Furthermore, he was a professional draftsman and industrial designer, which might indeed account for the compass this symbolic figure holds, but it does not account for the obviously faulty design of the Clément whose proportions are incorrectly drawn. Still, it's a striking poster whose central theme is pride of ownership and workmanship, qualities that Clément obviously wishes to instill in the potential buyer and which the artist — whoever he may be — aptly brings out.

66
Artist: Edward Penfield (1866-1925). Product: Orient Cycles. Year: c. 1895. Size 28 x 42 in. / 71 x 107 cm. Courtesy: The SandyVal Graphics Ltd. Collection.

Edward Penfield is best-known for the many small *Harper's Magazine* posters he designed for that periodical; they were more properly called window bills at the time. He produced about 75 such posters while he was art director of the monthly from 1891 to 1901. And it is these posters for *Harper's* which are exhibited and reproduced time and time again. It is therefore refreshing to be able to present two posters (see also the Northampton Bicycle poster, page 69) by Penfield which are not only different but which, more than the *Harper's* posters, show the true genius of the artist. In these and other posters, Penfield can be compared most favorably to Lautrec — his figures at once introspective and yet powerful, gathering their impact from a delicate balance in composition and the use of wide areas of flat colors. Bradley may be better known, but Penfield was the finest poster artist the United States has produced. Bradley himself indicated his debt to Penfield and gave one of the best descriptions of Penfield's contribution to poster art in his new publication, *Bradley: His Book* (see

58

59

60

61

62

63

64

65

66

notes to 24): "He is like a tree that is well rooted, and strong in every branch. We have seen its leaves and flowers; they have sweetened the atmosphere of art; and now there is the ruddy fruit, and when we forget posters as a craze and value them as art, as a medium through which the artist speaks, then the fruit will have mellowed and ripened, and we shall realize better than now, the thought, care and patience necessary to bring it to that stage. Mr. Penfield's work is wholly his own. It represents a thought; an expression; a mode of treatment which belongs to him alone; there is backbone to it. No matter what the pose, no matter what the idea, behind it all there is life, there is drawing, and good drawing. This alone marks him as a master; and in methods of reproduction, that difficult point to which so few give a passing thought, he is a past master."

As was the custom, this poster was printed for use by agents and retailers throughout the United States; the imprinting of the local address (in this case, for the Philadelphia agency of Waltham) was subsequently added.

67
Artist: Unknown. Product: Stoewer's Greif Bicycles. Year: c. 1900. Size: 21 x 35 in. / 54 x 89 cm. Courtesy: Staatsgalerie Baden-Württemberg, Stuttgart.

Here again a classical theme and popular academic style of the times are commercially applied by a poster artist. And what it lacks in design, as shown by later German posters, it makes up for in fine printing and interest of detail and theme. And the theme here is stated at the bottom of the poster: "Use the time! It passes by so quickly!" And there is a good deal of added symbolism here, some obvious (the hour-glass) and some only a little more subtle (the uprooted tree). Note that although her Stoewer is on a dirt road, it's not really dirt she's kicking up, but a fine cloud. Since she's just descended from the heavens on the light-weight Stoewer, that's only to be expected.

The company, Gebrüder Stoewer Fahrradfabrik of Stettin, was founded in 1899 and had a reputation for building quality bicycles. They later built motorcycles and automobiles. This poster, like the one on pages 64 and 70, was also printed by Grimme & Hempel of Leipzig.

68
Artist: Unknown. Product: Hurtu Bicycles. Year: c. 1900. Size: 44 x 59 in. / 112 x 150 cm. Courtesy: Bibliothèque Nationale, Paris.

Hurtu used this famous design in many of its posters, but this is believed to be the earliest version. As it introduced new bicycle models each year, it used the same design, changing not only the bicycle itself, but also altering slightly the dress (later versions have the lady's shoulders less "puffy" and the jacket more clearly delineated from the skirt, with buttons and belt added), and the composition (the rider is placed higher in the poster so that her hat covers the bottom right part of the "R" in Hurtu). Later posters, which were smaller in size, were printed by Verneau rather than Lemercier, and some omit "Diligeon" while others add language about new innovations, such as reinforced steel tubing. Throughout all the changes, the basic strength of this poster — the sharp contrast of black figure against solid yellow background — remains. Hurtu, one of the earliest bicycle manufacturers to go into automobiles, soon moved to Avenue de la Grande Armée with all the others.

69
Artist: Edward Penfield (1866-1925). Product: Northampton Bicyles. Year: c. 1895 Size: 27 x 36 in. / 69 x 91 cm. Courtesy: Private Collection.

Penfield's work has been commented on previously (66) and this beautiful poster for Northampton bicycles well illustrates the impact and power of this masterful artist. It is more the sure power of a revving engine than of actual movement; there is so much self-assurance in both content and style that one does not need proof of speed or even mobility. The composition, design and color are so perfect here that it's one of the

few posters of which it may be said that to move one line or change one shade would be unimaginable.

70
Artist: Unknown. Product: Opel Bicycles. Year: c. 1900. Size: 22 x 34 in. / 56 x 86 cm. Courtesy: Staatsgalerie Baden-Württemberg, Stuttgart.

Another fine poster by another unknown artist in the printing firm of Grimme & Hempel of Leipzig. The skill of this company is well-illustrated in this fine, four-color lithograph. The combination of large flat color areas with subtle use of overlapping color stones to provide fine details rivals that of Chéret's best printing. And one wants to give the title of The Winner ("Die Siegerin") to the design as much as to the intended bicycle brand. The bottom was left blank for later imprinting by local Opel agents.

The firm of Adam Opel of Russelsheim was one of the earliest German bicycle companies, founded in 1884. It stopped producing bicycles in 1938 and, like most manufacturers on both sides of the war, concentrated on armaments. From this date, automobiles were the only vehicles produced by Opel.

71
Artist: Unknown. Product: Meteor Bicycles. Year: c. 1900. Size: 18 x 28 in. / 46 x 70 cm. Courtesy: Staatsgalerie Baden-Württemberg, Stuttgart.

This is indeed a beautifully designed and executed poster in every sense. Although, as in all other posters, the lady is in the lead, it's the man who holds our attention. And what a man! Has there ever been such a "cool" character in the history of poster art? That pose of self-confidence, one arm in his pocket, and dressed — not to kill, since it's obvious that this man effortlessly and regularly conquers all, women and roads — but casually, with beret and turtle-neck sweater and pipe in mouth. The lady is also the picture of poise and "chic," but again, it's the self-assurance of the man which holds our grip. The "sunset glow" of the background adds to the romance. This poster is so good because it immediately grabs our attention and establishes a favorable mood for the sale of Meteor and yet it takes another look to realize how very deliberate all the component parts have been created and arranged. It's quite maddening not to be able to toast this artist by name. The printer is again Grimme & Hempel of Leipzig.

The artist decided not to leave a blank space at the bottom, for the later imprinting of the agent's name, but rather to extend the wall a little further down. As a result, most agents did not imprint their names, fearing they would not show up too well, and instead, pasted sheets below the name "Meteor" with their information on it, such as, in one version, "GUZZONI ANTONIO, representative for Trevis and nearby provinces."

Meteor was the bicycle brand of the firm of F. R. Langhan, Gewehr und Fahrradfabrik in Zella Mehlis, Thuringen, Germany, founded in 1894. After 1948 the company became Meteorwerke.

72
Artist: Fritz Schoen. (1871- ?) Product: Dürkopp Bicycles. Year: 1910. Size: 32 x 49 in. / 82 x 124 cm. Courtesy: Kunstgewerbemuseum, Zurich.

The style of this poster is quite different from that of the Dürkopp Bicycle poster which appears on page 45. It relies on humor rather than style. The copy reads, "Light and elegant . . . Can't be run into the ground!" Look ma, one finger.

73
Artist: George Moore. Product: Matador Cycles. Year: c. 1907. Size: 29 x 39 in. / 73 x 100 cm. Courtesy: Batavus Museum, Heerenveen, Holland.

This may well have been a "stock-art" poster by Moore which Temple Press, the London printer, then sold to bicycle manufacturers for their own usage. It is obvious that the blue lettering for both the bicycle brand name at the top and the Dutch company at the bottom were later imprinted, and there is no brand name on the bicycles themselves. Of chief interest in this poster is the

photographic style it shows, emphasizing both the dress of the day and the beautiful landscape to give a feeling of reality to the setting. We are also being sold on the idea that romance and nature beckon — but only with a bike. An earlier poster by Moore appears on page 35.

74
Artist: Rünckel. Product: Fongers Bicycles. Year: c. 1915. Size: 17 x 28 in. / 43 x 70 cm. Courtesy: Batavus Museum, Heerenveen, Holland.

This is a beautiful poster, with an unusual design that somehow works. The copy at the top reads "Fongers — the only bicycle!" It is not clear if the name of the store at the bottom was later imprinted or was part of the original press run, nor is it clear if "Rünckel" is the name of the poster workshop in The Hague or that of the artist.

The Fongers bicycle is one of the oldest trademarks of Holland and Queen Wilhelmina and after her, Queen Juliana, were frequently seen riding their Fongers bicycle. In 1971, Batavus took over this factory. Two other Fongers posters appear on pages 90 and 92.

This, and several other posters in this collection, were photographed at the Batavus Museum in Heerenveen, Holland. To see both the lovely countryside of Holland and to view one of the best collections of historic bicycles, motorcyles and automobiles, I would recommend a drive from Amsterdam to Heerenveen, which is about 30 km. (18 miles) south of Leeuwarden, in the northern part of the country. The ride over the Afsluitdijk, the dike which closes the former Zuyder Zee, to Groningen is quite breathtaking. The museum is open from May 1 to October 1, and a call ahead to check on hours is advisable.

75
Artist: Fritz Rehm (1871 - 1928). Product: Victoria Bicycles. Year: c. 1910. Size: 31 x 42 in. / 77 x 108 cm. Courtesy: Berghaus Verlag.

This is one of several beautiful posters for Victoria by Rehm. In another poster he uses a striking "Art Deco" style with a cyclist silhouetted against a bright yellow sky; here there is a more traditional and decorative approach, but his typography is always tastefully placed within the overall design. Rehm was an illustrator and designer of posters and books; he worked and lived in Munich all his life. Victoria was founded about 1888 and after World War II parts of it were taken over by Herkules, which is today the firm of Fichtel und Sachs in Schweinfurt and which still manufactures bicycles under the name of Herkules.

76
Artist: Plinio Codognato (1879-1940). Product: Pirelli Tires. Year: 1916. Size: 35 x 50 in. / 89 x 127 cm. Courtesy: Pirelli Tire Corporation.

The charm and personality of Codognato's work comes through beautifully in this poster for Pirelli Tires. Possibly because the model is the artist's son, this is one of the finest posters produced by him in a long and successful career. Codognato created posters for Cinzano, Liebig, Legnano, Bianchi and Frera, among others, and for twenty years he was the poster designer for Fiat, creating also "La Revista Fiat" (The Fiat Review.) He did many advertising illustrations and was active in the design of early mailing pieces.

Although time has faded and lightened it somewhat, the background was originally solid black, one of the earliest and largest lithographs to use solid black background.

The boy's clothes represent the colors of the Italian flag: green, white and red. The boy was used because Pirelli at this time and for the purposes of this poster wanted to emphasize its tires for children's bicycles. But it is interesting to note that if you cover everything except the face, the model might be mistaken for a pretty lady. The eyes are hard to resist; the attraction is immediate and total — it's a gorgeous poster.

Pirelli, with a long tradition of fine graphics and fine tires, remains today one of the leading quality manufacturers of bicycle tires. For a very different Pirelli design, see page 94.

77
Artist: Unknown. Product: Naumann Bicycles. Year: c. 1905. Size: 24 x 35 in. / 60 x 88 cm. Courtesy: Staatsgalerie Baden-Württemberg, Stuttgart.

Unlike some Art Nouveau posters which used flowers as a decorative border, this one places the flowers inside the design and uses bicycle wheels as the border motif. The copy reads: "Naumann's Bicycles are the best." Below that is the name of their distributor in the town of Reichenberg, Josef Hefter. The company was founded in Dresden about 1885 under the name of Seidel & Naumann and as with others stopped producing bicycles in 1936 to go into military production. The artist, who deserves much credit for this fine design, is unknown, but the printing firm was W. Hagelberg Akt. Ges., Berlin.

We see here again the deliberate use of a man's bicycle for the woman rider. Naumann's, of course, had women's bicycles with depressed top tube at the time. (A humorous 1896 poster for the firm shows a couple at a forest picnic, he inscribing his love for Naumann and its new pneumatic tire on a tree while she, seated with glass of wine in hand, looks so somewhat incredulously; her bike next to her is a woman's model). No doubt all companies were pushing men's bikes, which accounted for the bulk of sales, and in a one-bicycle family the woman with bloomers could handle such bike quite well. However, one also suspects that the horizontal bar makes a better parallel design element when combined with the entire frame structure of the bicycle. And here the geometric form of the tubular frame, unencumbered by spokes, is a major design element of the entire poster. There are others who might put forth some sexual connotations, but this should not be seriously considered.

78
Artist: Unknown. Product: Adler Bicycles. Year: c. 1910. Size: 17 x 29 in. / 44 x 73 cm. Courtesy: Staatsgalerie Baden-Württemberg, Stuttgart.

With this poster for Adler, we enter into a new era of poster design, leaving the Art Nouveau and fin-de-siècle exoticism and splashy color we have seen elaborated in many previous examples and ushering a more stark, simple and representational approach to poster art, shortly leading to what has become known as "Art Deco" and later to "Bauhaus" styles. Some of the hallmarks of this new style — the use of perspective, the broad color plains, the integration of word and image —were hinted at in the Penfield posters and are even more pronounced in this striking poster for Adler. The artist's use of the bicycle frame itself as a design element, noted above in comments on the Naumann poster, is even more clearly and forcefully delineated here. The printer of the poster is Kunst-Anstalt Kornsand & Co., Frankfurt.

The firm of Adler, founded in 1880 and noted for its high quality, specialized in touring bikes and later built a Berg und Talrad (mountain and valley bike) with multiple gears. They stopped bicycle production in 1954, concentrating on such things as sewing machines and typewriters.

79
Artist: Leonetto Cappiello (1875-1942). Product: Lefort Tires. Year: 1911. Size: 46 x 62 in. / 117 x 157 cm. Courtesy: Bibliothèque Nationale, Paris.

Although humor was often an integral part of Cappiello's art, this large and droll poster — the mice break their teeth trying to eat through "the strong" (Lefort) tires — is not typical of the lively designs, bold colors, and simple forms which made him such a popular poster artist from 1900 to about 1915. Although frequently compared to Chéret because of his use of women in almost all his posters, the style is much more expressive of Lautrec's and at his best Cappiello could well match the master's flair. He moved to Paris from his native Italy while still young and began drawing caricatures for periodicals; his work for *Le Rire*, beginning in 1898, is classic.

80
Artist: Louis Oury. Product: Kosmos Tires. Year: c. 1900. Size: 48 x 33 in. / 122 x 85 cm. Courtesy: Private Collection.

Another humorous bicycle tire poster, this one is typical of the cartoon style of Oury. The policeman comes on the scene asking "What's going on here again?" and the crowd replies, "Officer, we're admiring the marvelous Kosmos tires." Oury did several posters for Kosmos, all using this witty caricature style. Probably the funniest one shows a disheveled man with brief case broken and papers strewn on the Champs Elysées and a crowd gathering around him as the lady cyclist who has just ridden over him asks, "Have I hurt you, Sir?" And he replies, "No, young lady, on the contrary, for you use Kosmos tires, don't you?" She admits, "Yes, Sir, it's the most practical one," to which he gives her the great assurance, "I noticed that immediately; it is so supple and so soft."

In almost all these posters, whether for Kosmos or the Grand Manège Velócipédique, Oury uses the vertical bars shown here. Why this should be is difficult to understand. There can be no reason for it from a lithographical point of view; it does not enhance the design but rather detracts from it. Possibly he wishes us to look out and see the crowd as if we were inside a café looking at crowds outside the window. He was a sculptor also, and possibly he sought to give his posters a three-dimensional feeling, or at least one of depth. But none of these speculations is quite satisfactory.

The facial expressions and the dress are also of interest in this crowd scene; the lady at the left is the kind often seen in a poster by Georges de Feure. As indicated on the tire itself, Kosmos was the French licensee of Dunlop.

81
Artist: Unknown. Product: Crown Bicycles. Year: 1895. Size: 21 x 16 in. / 53 x 41 cm. Courtesy: Library of Congress, Washington.

This poster, executed at the height of the American bicycle as well as poster craze, shows us much about both. The manufacturer is intent on showing the lightness of his new tubular-steel, chain-driven, pneumatic-tired bicycle; note that the little girl single-handedly lifts not her little girl's model but her father's bicycle. And bicycle makers also wanted to stress the fun-for-the-whole-family approach as well as indicate to the viewer that he, like the persons in the poster, can escape the maddening crowds of the city and discover the wonders and tranquility of nature. The good life is at hand — with the help of your Crown Cycle.

It also shows us that, until some of the few good American poster artists of the time came along (such as Bradley, Reed, Penfield, Parrish and Rhead) most of the poster art of the United States was of a realistic, almost photographic style (see

also pages 49 and 61). And while the quality of workmanship (here a five-color lithograph) is high and the poster often gives us a good glimpse of the times, these are usually not memorable or striking. Collectors waited for more decorative and artistic posters to come along.

82
Artist: Unknown. Product: Waffenrad Bicycles. Year: 1902. Size: 24 x 40 in. / 61 x 102 cm. Courtesy: Staatsgalerie Baden-Württemberg, Stuttgart.

Manufacturers in all countries pushed the military uses of bicycles from the 1880's until World War II. The French Captain Gerard is usually credited as the first designer of light, foldable military bicycles with solid snap and clamp locks. In France, the Morel company led the way in the 1880's, followed soon by German firms such as Adler and Viktoria, as well as British, Italian and American firms. The bicycles were quite light, most were collapsible, and many had military accessories as well. The Pope Company, for instance, mounted a Colt automatic machine gun on its proposed models for the United States Army. Much later, British (BSA) and Japanese manufacturers built models for paratroopers; German troops marched into Poland, cyclists pulled by cars in front of them with rope; Canadian soldiers went ashore on D-Day with their bicycles, and, more recently, American troops were dumbfounded by the Vietnamese guerillas' ability to move troops and supplies through mountains and jungles by means of bicycles. That arms know no boundary, especially if profits can be made, is graphically demonstrated by Mr. Gerd Volke, who will show the visitor to his bicycle collection in Düsseldorf identical parts of military bicycles from various countries: It is clear, for instance, that the handlebar on the German "Express" built by Adler is the same handlebar used on the military bicycles from France and Italy. Many of the technical improvements in bicycles came via its military uses.

There are many posters depicting the bicycle at war, both as a courier and a fighting instrument. Waffenrad, the Austrian Arms Manufacturer, began in 1887 under the name of Steyr. From 1935 to 1957 the name was Steyr-Daimler Puch, A.G., and today it is Junioren Werke. In this richly colored poster, it's not only the military advantages that are being promoted. The printer was Leutert & Schneiderwind of Dresden.

83
Artist: J. Cardona. Product: Rambler Cycles. Year: 1901. Size: 37 x 51 in. / 94 x 130 cm. Courtesy: Bibliothèque Nationale, Paris.

We have seen the bicycle wheel used as a decorative motif before (see pages 63 and 77), but here the artist, who appears to be "J. Cardona," uses it as part of the fabric design of the elegantly-dressed allegorical woman. (There was an illustrator working in Paris at this time by the name of Juan Cardona, but I am not sure that he is the designer of this poster; his signature, as it appears in journals, is different from the one on this poster.)

Rambler was at this time the brand name of the Gormully & Jeffery Manufacturing Company of Chicago. But with the bicycle slump of the early 1900's — production in the United States went from 2,000,000 in 1897 to 250,000 in 1904 — many firms closed, including this one, and the brand name of Rambler was taken over by the Pope Manufacturing Company of Hartford, Connecticut, about 1903. Pope also produced bicycles under the name of Columbia and Ideal. This poster was printed in France, probably for Lucien Charmet, the Paris agent for Rambler and Rudge, who used to advertise these as "Les 2 Grandes Marques adoptées par tous les Cyclists connaisseurs." (The two largest makes, used by all knowledgeable riders).

84

Artist: Ballerio. Product: Bianchi Bicycles. Year: c. 1905. Size: 39 x 85 in. / 100 x 215 cm. Courtesy: Edoardo Bianchi Velo, Milan.

This huge poster was printed in three sheets and shows the influence of French poster art on the Italians of this period. Italians were early to catch on to the appeal and variety made possible in lithographic posters (as opposed to letterpress, largely type-only posters). This was largely due to the efforts of the Ricordi company which installed the latest printing equipment it had found in Germany and developed the poster processes being used in France and began, in the 1890's, to turn out a large quantity of very fine posters. This poster, however, was produced by another printer in Milan. Note the ghost-like appearance of the automobile in the background; Bianchi produced motorcycles and automobiles as well as bicycles with a reputation for excellent craftsmanship. The text inside the front wheel indicates that Bianchi is the "Supplier to the Royal House."

85

Artist: A. Forchey. Product: Presto Bicycles. Year: c. 1905. Size: 24 x 32 in. / 60 x 82 cm. Courtesy: Bibliothèque Nationale, Paris.

Many early bicycle posters had a bet-you-can't-catch-me theme to emphasize their speed. For instance, a Racycle poster produced in 1899 by the Miami Cycle Company of Ohio showed a calm, pipe-smoking gentleman with desert hat pedaling ahead of a chasing group of Arabian stallions with their threatening nomadic riders. A later Raleigh poster shows a cyclist at first pursued and then winning his race against a fierce lion. And so it went. But this has to be one of the most extreme and funniest of the lot: The hobo, without use of hands or feet, is able to keep ahead of that new contraption called the airplane, recently invented by a couple of bicycle mechanics from Ohio by the name of Wright. The text reads: "Without motor, without wings and . . . just as fast, with the Presto Bicycle."

86

Artist: Markous. Product: Cottereau Bicycles. Year: c. 1905. Size: 31 x 45 in. / 78 x 114 cm. Courtesy: Batavus Museum, Heerenveen, Holland.

The artist, whose name appears to be "Markous," has used a very fine, pencil-like approach to his drawing and given his subject a feeling of quiet elegance within broad impressionistic lines. Cottereau Bicycles were manufactured in Dijon.

87

Artist: Daan Hoeksema (1879 - ?) Product: Simplex Bicycles. Year: 1907. Size: 21 x 44 in. / 53 x 112 cm. Courtesy: Libreria Milano Libri.

It is hard to define a Dutch style of poster art, but if it has any special indigenous quality it is an insistence on realism and direct portrayal, a no-nonsense approach that leaves no room for exotic, wild or surrealistic treatment. Hoeksema's fine poster for Simplex has a classical simplicity which makes it quite compelling. His posters are totally devoid of embellishment or clutter and he is only interested in the most basic and "cleanest" form possible to portray his message.

The copy at the top announces that Simplex has 70% less friction. The Simplex brand was bought by N. V. Gazelle Rijwielfabriek, in Dieren, Holland. Another Simplex poster appears on page 89.

88

Artist: Mich. Product: Hutchinson Tires. Year: c. 1920. Size: 31 x 46 in. / 80 x 118 cm. Courtesy: Kunstgewerbemuseum, Zurich.

This famous figure by Mich became a trademark for Hutchinson and was seen in many posters and advertisements for many years. Even this one poster design was used over and over by the company: In this one the droll rider's garb is white polka dots on blue cloth; on others it was white on red, and the background of the poster might be blue instead of yellow as here. The tire would change only slightly; here there are spokes, in others there would be none. But always the same figure with this faithful dog and the slogan at the top: Stronger than Steel ("Plus solide que l'Acier").

In 1853 an American engineer, Hiram Hutchinson, went to France to exploit a license for the vulcanization of rubber. His first factory at Langlée, which then specialized in making galoshes, is still there but has grown quite a bit, now employing 2,500 workers. There are also plants in Germany, Spain and Italy, but most of the bike tires are made at the large Langlée plant.

89

Artist: F. Hart-Nibbrig. Product: Simplex Bicycles. Year: c. 1912. Size: 33 x 45 in. / 83 x 115 cm. Courtesy: Batavus Museum, Heerenveen, Holland.

Leave the hot, congested city of Amsterdam and ride into the quiet, green countryside. No, that's not the copy, but that's the clear and simple message of this poster. The actual copy — Simplex/Quick/Strong — is too powerful for the placid scene depicted here. As anyone who has visited Holland knows, it has the highest per-capita consumption of bicycles in the world. The sight of bicycles everywhere leaves as much of an impression on the American tourist as the canals and the Rembrandts.

90

Artist: F. G. Schlette. Product: Fongers Bicycles. Year: c. 1915. Size: 32 x 89 in. / 81 x 227 cm. Courtesy: Batavus Museum, Heerenveen, Holland.

This poster is imposing chiefly because of its almost life-like size, over seven feet high! The copy reads: "Used in the Dutch and Dutch-Indian Army." Another treatment of the military uses of the bicycle can be seen on page 82 (Waffenrad) and another treatment of the Fongers sales pitch can be seen on pages 74 and 92.

91

Artist: Raoul Vion. Product: Sanpene Bicycle. Year: c. 1925. Size: 31 x 46 in. / 80 x 118 cm. Courtesy: Bibliothèque Nationale, Paris.

If traveling faster than an airplane is the ultimate statement of a bicycle's claim to speed, then this poster must be the ultimate (or most ludicrous) claim for its comfort. This was typical of posters of the period: Many showed cyclists riding down stairs with great ease while others combined the two elements, so that one poster depicts a young lady on a bicycle racing far ahead of an oncoming train — on the train tracks. "Sans peine" means without difficulty, or easily, and the Sanpene Bicycle is meant to connote this. The poster announces that it is equipped with shock absorber and recuperator. "It gives you legs — Eliminates vibrations." Everyone in this five-color lithograph seems quite happy and satisfied, except the incredulous dog who's just been run over.

92

Artist: Unknown. Product: Fongers Bicycles. Year: c. 1920. Size: 16 x 33 in. / 40 x 83 cm. Courtesy: Batavus Museum, Heerenveen, Holland.

There is a photographic quality to this richly colored and detailed poster. The colors of the three ladies' blouses — red, white and purple — are especially vivid. One would like to give praise to the lithographer, as well as the artist, but the poster was hung by a wooden clamp bar at top and bottom which could not be removed, and thus their identity is probably covered up. As previously noted (74), Fongers was taken over by Batavus in 1971.

93

Artist: H.W. Event: Bike-Ball Game. Year: 1947. Size: 36 x 50 in. / 90 x 125 cm. Courtesy: Kunstgewerbemuseum, Zurich.

Bike-Ball is a popular game in many European countries and it's almost as old as the bicycle itself. The game is usually held indoors, in some gymnastics auditorium or large hall, but can be played most anywhere. Each team has two players, one at the goal and the other in the field. The game has two 15-minute periods. The wide appeal of the game is indicated by the many countries which participated in the 1973 world championships held in Germany: Belgium, France, Germany, Italy, Sweden, Czechoslovakia, Austria, Switzerland, Denmark, and, for the first time in European competition, Japan. Bike-Ball is not yet an Olympic sport and it is still totally unknown in the United States. Possibly the renewed interest in the bicycle itself will bring the game here shortly. American television executives: Are you listening? The poster, by an artist whose initials are "H.W.", promotes a 1947 match in Basel, Switzerland.

94

Artist: Engelmann. Product: Pirelli Tires. Year: 1952. Size: 27 x 39 in. / 69 x 100 cm. Courtesy: Kunstgewerbemuseum, Zurich.

Well, here's an artist who certainly wasn't afraid of tire spokes! His very bold use of them as an integral part of the design makes for an effective poster. It was printed by photo-offset in two colors, the word "Pirelli" being white inside a red background; the remainder of the poster, art and type, is black. The copy at the bottom: "The tire for everyone." Another Pirelli poster is shown on page 76.

95

Artist: Luis Velez. Product: Windsor Bicycles. Year: 1971. Size: 20 x 26 in. / 50 x 66 cm. Courtesy: Acer-Mex, S.A.

This is an effective design and one of two posters in this book printed by silk-screen process. (See also page 101). The word "Mexico" at top and the bottom line of text are in red; the name "Windsor" and the border area above and below it are in blue; the rest, including the art work, is all stark black on white background. Windsor Bicycles are manufactured by Acer-Mex, S.A., of Mexico; this 25-year-old firm also produces motorcycles and in addition to domestic marketing also sells its bikes in the United States and Canada.

96

Agency: Integral Propaganda Tecnica Ltd. Product: Caloi Bicycles. Year: 1972. Size: 37 x 25 in. / 93 x 63 cm. Courtesy: Bicicletas Caloi S/A.

This is the first example of a photographic poster in this book, and it should, once and for all, end the nonsense that photographic posters lack artistic merit. Printed in four-color offset lithography, this poster advertises the Dobravel brand of the Caloi Company, Brazil's leading maker of bicycles and an exporter to many countries around the world. It is interesting to note that the bicycle's opportunity for freedom of movement ("A Sua Independencia") is still being stressed today just as it was almost 100 years ago. And since you have been looking at the details of this fine product, you have no doubt noticed that this is also the first example here of a folding bicycle. These small-wheeled, collapsible bicycles have become very popular the past few years and they are probably a reflection of increased urbanization and the shortage of storage space such living affords.

In crediting a poster produced by an advertising agency, the art director and, in this case, the

96

photographer, should properly be mentioned. Unfortunately, I was not able to get this information. The agency, Integral Propaganda Tecnica Ltd., like Caloi, is located in Sao Paulo.

97
Artist: Carl Moos (1878 - ?) Product: Maxim Bicycles. Year: c. 1912. Size: 24 x 35 in. / 62 x 88 cm. Courtesy: Staatsgalerie Baden-Württemberg, Stuttgart.

German posters of this period are among the best ever created, with strong and linear composition, uncluttered design, and excellent integration of type and image. Carl Moos was one of the most prolific of posterists of that period, being also a painter, lithographer and sculptor. All of his posters were printed by Vereinigte Druckereien of Munich, where he founded with five others, "Die 6," a group of poster artists who banned together and did all their work at this printing plant. (Vereinigte is also the printer of the famous 1912 Munich Zoo poster by Hohlwein, who was not a member of "The Six.") Most of his posters, executed between 1907 and 1914, were done for local retail shops in Munich and he did not get the wide recognition his work deserves.

Maxim Bicycles, founded in 1893 by Franz Bieber of Munich, were of the highest quality, but production stopped about 1928. They were never mass producers and, in fact, had a reputation for being something of the "Rolls Royce" of Bicycles. You could order white-walled or bright-red-walled tires, instead of the usual drab black tires. That it was the bicycle of the "smart set" is well indicated in this poster.

98
Artist: Unknown. Product: Stern Bicycles. Year: c. 1913. Size: 18 x 30 in. / 45 x 75 cm. Courtesy: Staatsgalerie Baden-Württemberg, Stuttgart.

The ghost-like riders descending from the Stars ("Stern") make an interesting design, and the composition and color combinations are quite effective. But this could also have a disturbing theme — Cyclists returning from the dead to haunt the city at night — which might not enhance the sale of the product. The printer (J. C. Konig & Ebhardt of Hannover, who also had a firm in Berlin by the name of Reuter & Siecke) is well known for the fine posters he printed for leading German artists such as Buhe, Edel and Hohlwein. But there is no indication of this poster's designer.

99
Artist: Ludwig Hohlwein (1874-1949). Product: Torpedo Bicycles. Year: 1921. Size: 19 x 30 in. / 48 x 77 cm. Courtesy: Kunstgewerbemuseum, Zurich.

Hohlwein was probably the greatest of the German poster artists before World War II. (The greatest German poster artist since then, working in a completely different style, is Gunther Kieser.) He is most closely identified with the "Art Deco" school of poster art. He did several posters for Torpedo Bicycles, all of which throw geometric color forms on the background of a cyclist or group of cyclists as if they were so many discarded cards from a playing deck. It is attention-getting and the composition is interesting, but it's not Hohlwein at his most effective. He is best known for his Munich Zoo poster of 1912, his many World War I posters, and his 1936 Olympic poster. He was an architect and interior designer as well, but from 1906, his main preoccupation was with the hundreds of poster commissions he received.

100
Artist: Jean Carlu (b. 1900). Product: Peugeot Bicycles. Year: 1922. Size: 24 x 31 in. / 60 x 80 cm. Courtesy: Kunstgewerbemuseum, Zurich.

This is a difficult poster to place, stylistically and historically. The motif is strictly turn-of-the-century and yet the force of the bronze-statue-like woman holding up, for all the world to see, the latest Peugeot model, with a red pattern (is that the tail-end of the fiery streak she has left behind

in her descent to earth?) against an ominous blue sky — all these indicate an artist in transition and portends a style not yet fully realized. For this is not a typical Carlu poster. The artist is much better known for his cubistic, Cassandre-like posters of sharp geometric planes and bold use of typography. His best-known posters, done for the Office of Emergency Management during World War II, after he had moved to the United States, are "Give 'em both Barrels" (Machine gun and rivet are paralleled in design and intent; 1941) and "America's Answer! Production" (A worker's glove, wrench grasped, turning to the "o" in "production" which has become a nut; 1942). The bold draftsmanship which made Carlu famous is not yet realized here: Although this poster has a certain compelling quality, it invites "too much" rather than "touché!"

Peugeot, which started in the bicycle business in 1886, has enjoyed a continuing reputation for fine craftsmanship and its bicycles are very much in demand in the United States right now.

101
Artist: Hiroshi Ohchi (b. 1908). Product: Miyata Bicycles. Year: 1958. Size: 28 x 40 in. / 72 x 102 cm. Courtesy: The artist.

This poster was created for the 70th Anniversary of Miyata Works, Ltd., one of the oldest and largest manufacturers of bicycles in Japan, producing cycles under the brand names of Miyata and Mister. Its plant in Chigasaki City, outside of Toyko, is one of the largest in the world and has a capacity of building over 50,000 bicycles each month. In spite of this, the company remains unknown to Americans since it does not export to the United States, no doubt due to the relatively higher price of this quality line. Miyata is part of the Panasonic group.

Hiroshi Ohchi is one of Japan's leading designers and, as an editor of the graphic magazine, *Idea* and as a teacher of art and industrial design, he has had a great influence on an entire generation of Japanese artists. In most of his posters, he shows a great ability to combine photography with modern design elements, such as in his posters for the Don Cossack Chorus (1952) or another for Miyata Motorcycles (1960). But three of his most effective posters have been pure design and pure delight: There is a 1957 Hirodi Bicycle poster which uses the bicycle as a basic design element in a way seldom seen before; a 1961 silk-screened poster for Miyata Bicycles, made of bold geometric forms and colors; and the third one is presented in this volume. This poster is one of only two posters printed by silk-screen process reproduced in this book (see Windsor, page 95).

It has been a bit disquieting to see the Japanese, who were in many ways the inventors of the pictorial poster and certainly the inspiration to so many of Europe's and America's finest poster artists, produce banal and pedestrian poster designs for the past thirty years. Most represent a vague attempt to "westernize" the product with a "psychedelic" flavor and thus wind up being the worst of all worlds. Ohchi is one of the few shining examples of the exception to the rule; he carries a proud tradition proudly.

102
Artist: Unknown. Product: Cosmos Bicycles. Year: 1935. Size: 36 x 50 in. / 90 x 128 cm. Courtesy: Kunstgewerbemuseum, Zurich.

There has been much said and written about the "Swiss school" of poster design, the tradition most associated with designs such as those produced by Herbert Leupin or Celestino Piatti, two of Switzerland's finest artists. But this poster predates this period and, except for its light-hearted attitude toward the product, is not typical of this "school." But nonetheless, it's a fine poster. And since one does not know the name of the artist, it is well to reflect on the fact that much credit must be given to Swiss printers whose encouragement and fine craftsmanship have played such large part in making "Swiss

posters" synonymous with "good posters." The three largest and best firms in the poster printing business there are those of Wassermann in Basel, J. E. Wolfensberger in Zurich, and the printer of this Cosmos poster, J. C. Muller of Zurich also. Cosmos Bicycles founded in 1894, are manufactured by B. Schild & Cie., AG, of Biel, Switzerland.

103
Artist: Klöcker. Event: World Bicycle Championships. Year: 1936. Size: 36 x 50 in. / 91 x 128 cm. Courtesy: Kunstgewerbemuseum, Zurich.

This is a fascinating poster, much more from the point of history than of design. The artist's very linear approach and use of forceful perspective has kept it from being a cluttered design; it's still too busy, but somehow it works. But it's the juxtaposition of the flags of France, the United States, The Third Reich and Japan, among others, that is quite startling to come upon today. It was indicative, however, of the worldwide popularity of bicycle racing. Although cycling has attained the status of an Olympic sport, there is no relationship between this 1936 Championship held in Switzerland and the 1936 Olympic Games held in Germany. These championships were held every four years also and before the War they coincided with the Olympic years.

There were both amateur and professional competitions. The main attraction for amateur racers was the 145 km (90 miles) race, consisting of 20 laps around the Bremgarten Forest in Bern: 42 cyclists representing 12 countries started and 26 finished; the winner was Buchwalder of Switzerland in the time of 3.58.01, for an average speed of 36,7 km (about 23 miles) per hour. The professionals were required to go 30 laps, a distance of 220 km (136 miles); 39 cyclists from 12 countries participated and the winner was Antonin Magne of France in 5.53.32, for an average speed 37,06 km (again about 23 miles) per hour.

104
Artists: Behrmann & Bosshard. Product: Schwalbe Bicycles. Year: 1938. Size: 35 x 50 in. / 90 x 128 cm. Courtesy: Kunstgewerbemuseum, Zurich.

This poster shows the Bauhaus influence on artists of the period and is typical of the best of Swiss posters of that time — sparse, simple and yet bold and compelling. Schwalbe took pride in its light-weight bicycles and so the brand name and symbol of the bird ("Swallow") are effectively portrayed. "It's a smart bike" and a smart poster design. This one, like the one reproduced on pages 102 and 106, was printed by J. C. Muller of Zurich.

105
Artist: Unknown. Product: Kynoch Cycles. Year: c. 1923. Size: 40 x 60 in. / 102 x 152 cm. Courtesy: Victoria & Albert Museum, London.

Neither the artist nor printer's name appears on this poster in the Victoria & Albert Museum. It's an imposing poster, largely due to its size, which makes the rider seem life-like, coming straight at us. Although this poster, like so many others in this collection, makes the point that with the bicycle the wonders of nature (here the beauty of the English countryside) are open to us, there is also a strong feeling that the manufacturer wanted to remind women of the liberating effect their machines would have for them. There is also the intimation that not all roads or all beautiful things are open to the automobile,

106
Artist: Alex W. Diggelmann. Event: World Bicycle Championships. Year: 1953. Size: 35 x 50 in. / 90 x 128 cm. Courtesy: Kunstgewerbermuseum, Zurich.

Diggelmann did posters for several of the World Championships, always using the color stripes and the same "cyclist" motif. It's difficult to pick his best one; they're all uniformly excellent. One of the things which makes posters fascinating and different from other art forms is their problem-

solving aspect and it's most interesting to see how different artists approach the same subject, or "solve" the same "problem." Klöcker (*103*) and Diggelmann both want to indicate that it's indeed a "World" Championship and that cyclists from all over the world will be participating. Klöcker's solution, although historically interesting, is inferior to that of Diggelmann who shows us what fine poster design is all about.

The "Steher" and Sprint races were held in a stadium in Zurich. In "Steher" races the bicycle follows a motorcycle. The sprint, a pure speed contest, was won by Arie v. Fliet of Holland. The road contests for professionals and amateurs took place in Lugano. The professional race, in which 70 cyclists representing 12 nations competed in a 270 km (169 miles) course, was the first world championship won by Fausto Coppi of Italy, in 7.30.59, or an average speed of 36,78 km (about 23 miles) per hour. Coppi, then 34, went on to win many other championships and became the idol of European cycling. Kübler, who later became a Swiss national hero and won many championships including the "Tours" of France, Italy and Switzerland, first placed in a world's championship in this race, coming in seventh. An Italian, R. Filippi, also won the amateur event.

107
Artist: Hugo Koszler (b. 1900). Product: Semperit Tires. Year: 1950. Size: 23 x 33 in. / 59 x 84 cm. Courtesy: Semperit Aktiengesellschaft, Vienna.

This design appeared repeatedly in Semperit advertisements throughout Europe. It was first done as a four-color offset-lithograph poster as shown here and then a line-conversion was made from it for black-and-white letterpress advertisements in newspapers and magazines. In the advertisements, the words "Atelier Koszler" appears where there is now just a rubbed-out line in the upper left hand corner; the initials "JD" do not appear in these advertisements. Koszler is a Czechoslovakian-born artist who came to Vienna and established his own advertising agency, Friliko, about 1930. His studio is still active there. The "JD" at the bottom right stands for Josef Drewatulisch, who used to work at the Atelier Koszler before moving to the United States. So it's not altogether clear who gets credit for this lively design.

Semperit is a manufacturer of tires and tubes, not only for bicycles, but also for cars, tractors and other vehicles. A good deal of their sales are for bicycle parts exported to numerous countries in Europe and overseas.

108
Artist: Maciej Urbaniec. Event: Prague-Warsaw-Berlin International Peace Race. Year: 1966. Size: 24 x 38 in. / 67 x 97 cm. Courtesy: Kunstgewerbemuseum, Zurich.

Urbaniec has been one of the many Polish artists who have made that country so famous in the field of poster art, especially since World War II. His style is more abstract and more graphic than some of his contemporaries, such as Janowski (*110*), who use a more cartoon and lighthearted approach to their subject matter. Urbaniec has created many circus posters as well as posters for athletic events.

There have been two directions to posters in the past thirty years. One is to use photo-offset lithography to simply reproduce photograhic posters (actual photographs, such as *112*, or photo-like reproductions, such as *109*) and the other, more hopeful trend, as seen here, is to use the artist's paint brush with full authority and sweep without being inhibited by technique: Photo-offset (with few exceptions) will reproduce whatever the artist creates. While some feel that only the older method of stone lithography, with the artist being his own lithographer, is the true or more artistic way to do a poster, this is a mystique to be quickly dispelled: The artist is now more free to express himself and his responsibilities have increased as his options of expression have increased. It is, after all, the artist's vision and solution — the final product — which counts, and not the technical methods used to achieve it. What some artists have done with this new freedom is to take the low road of "psychedelic" mazes which are meant to confuse and confound the viewer, the antithesis of a poster's function. Others, have taken the high road: The end product of this graphic approach is quite excellent. The feeling of tension and speed of the race are well conveyed by Urbaniec's seemingly hurried, rough strokes of the brush. An American painter, Bob Cunningham, has also used this somewhat abstract style effectively in Football and Horseracing posters.

109
Artist: Shree Des Raj. Product: Atlas Bicycles. Year: 1971. Size: 20 x 30 in. / 51 x 76 cm. Courtesy: The Atlas Cycle Industries, Ltd.

At first glance this would appear to be a photograph, but in fact it is a five-color offset lithograph of a painting with very photographic qualities. One's attention is immediately riveted to the eyes and face of this beautiful rider: after that, the bicycle has to compete with the wonders of India's charming countryside. If this poster was produced for domestic use, then possibly it might have some very bold connotations to Indian women, both in new dress and travel options. Atlas is the largest producer and seller of bicycles in India and exports sizeable quantities to 35 countries abroad.

110
Artist: Witold Janowski. Product: Polish bikes. Year: 1972. Size: 25 x 33 in. / 64 x 84 cm. Courtesy: Universal Foreign Trade Enterprise, Warsaw.

Janowski is one of the most prolific of contemporary Polish artists, best known for his many circus posters (something obligatory for all artists from that country, but reaching its zenith in this master's hands) and his style can best be described as the style of "Joy!" That's the unifying element in all his work. Universal would seem to be the export arm of Poland's bicycle industry, its products being especially popular in the United States, Canada, Sweden and many other countries. All their posters carry the theme, "I Like Polish Bike!" and although widely different in graphic approach, they are uniformly excellent. If the response to be elicited by the viewer is meant to be "Me too" then this Janowski design certainly accomplishes that.

111
Artist: David Lance Goines (b. 1945). Company: Velo-Sport Bicycle Store, Berkeley, California. Year: 1970. Size: 18 x 24 in. / 46 x 61 cm. Courtesy: Private Collection.

David Lance Goines is a young American artist of enormous, though still largely unrecognized talent. His work is difficult to classify or describe. It is interesting that while many young posterists in America have reverted to an Art Nouveau (at its worst) style of elaboration and decorative, almost labyrinthian, overstatement, Goines seems to find his inspiration in the simpler "Art Deco" and subsequent Bauhaus style of the 30's. There is a formalism in all his work as well as a high degree of typographical sophistication. His best posters were created for the Pacific Film Archives in Berkeley. The poster shown here was first produced in 1970 for a bicycle shop in Berkeley which specializes in racing and touring equipment. It was printed in three-color photo-offset lithography — Goines himself did the camerawork, stripping and all presswork — in an edition of 3,000 copies of which 13 were signed (one being reproduced here); then in 1972, he brought out a second edition of 2,000 copies, printed in five colors (although this does not change the appearance at all) and signed in the plate, with slight text alteration at bottom, of which 100 were signed. I take second to no one in my admiration of this artist's work, yet I find this particular poster design somewhat disturbing: Although it can be enjoyed from the point of pure design, there is the question of what message the artist is trying to convey. If the pollution-free bicycle is meant to be contrasted to choking smoke of our environment, this doesn't do it. In the first place, the cyclists are obviously caught up in the middle of it, even if not the cause of it. And at a time when those concerned with the environment want to encourage mass transit rather than the more dangerous automobiles, it is the train which is seemingly made the culprit here,

Born in 1945 in Grant's Pass, Oregon, Goines, the eldest of eight children, apprenticed as a printing pressman at the age of 19. His interest in design and calligraphy matured from that point, until his skills as a printer and his ability as a designer allowed him to produce posters and books on a full-time professional basis. He founded Saint Heironymous Press in Berkeley. His first book was "An Introduction to the Elements of Calligraphy" (1968), then a yet unpublished new "Abecedarium" (1968) and "A Basic Formal Hand" (1970) and "Thirty Recipes for Framing" (1970). One of the handsomest catalogues ever produced — with Goines as pressman, of course — was Saint Heironymous Press' Catalogue for the May 1973 Exhibition of Goines posters at "The Poster," a San Francisco gallery devoted to original posters and related original-edition graphics.

112
Agency: Fleet Illustrating Ltd., London. Product: Raleigh Bicycles. Year: 1972. Size: 30 x 19 in. / 75 x 48 cm. Courtesy: Raleigh Industries Ltd.

This current poster for Raleigh industries shows the full potential of the photographic poster and should help dispel fears that photographic posters and photo-offset lithography to reproduce them, have in some way hindered the progress of poster art — or, as some snobs in the gallery and so-called-limited-edition graphics world would have you believe, has ended the art form forever. This poster combines all the good attributes which W. S. Rogers, previously quoted, demanded of an effective poster. Regrettably, publication time of the book occurred before I could find out the name of the art director, designer or photographer responsible for this poster. No doubt, Raleigh is "showing the flag" to remind its customers, at a time of fierce competition from Japan and the Far East, that it's a "British-made" and therefore better-made and superior product.

Raleigh is today the world's largest producer and exporter of bicycles as well as components and accessories that go with them. It has come a long way since Frank Bowden bought a small workshop in Raleigh Street, Nottingham, where in 1887, twelve men toiled to produce three high-wheelers per week. Raleigh bicycles were exhibited in the 1888 Stanley Show and by 1900, Bowden had built the largest cycle factory in the world, turning out 12,000 bicycles per year. There then followed a successive number of take-overs and amalgamations, beginning with the purchase in 1902 of the Sturmey and Archer variable gear; in 1932 the cycle interests of Humber Limited were acquired; in 1943 Rudge-Whitworth Company, in 1953 the Triumph Cycle Company, in 1957 B.S.A. Cycles Ltd., and in 1960 the racing specialists, Carlton Cycles Ltd. When in 1960 Raleigh itself was gobbled up by its parent company, Tube Investments Groups, it automatically inherited such famous bicycle names as Phillips, Hercules, Sun and Norman, and in the components field, Brooks and Lycett. During World War II it was the largest commercial supplier to the Armed Forces. Partly due to competition of low cost models, especially from Japan, output fell in the 1950's by 50%, from four to two million units. In 1965 it launched the small-wheel bicycle (the RSW 16) and in 1967 the business of Moulton Bicycles was amalgamated with Raleigh. Its "Chopper" model, introduced in 1970, proved especially popular with youngsters in the United States, it being the nearest thing to a motorcycle that a ten-year-old could ride. Raleigh, one of the major sponsors of the World Cycling Championships at Leicester in 1970, saw its teams and products win the Gold Medal for the one km. Sprint and the 5 km. Pursuit. A substantial amount of the company's export is directed to the United States and to take advantage of the bicycle craze here and help ward off competition from Japan and local manufacturers it is presently building a huge assembly plant in the midwest.

105

106

107

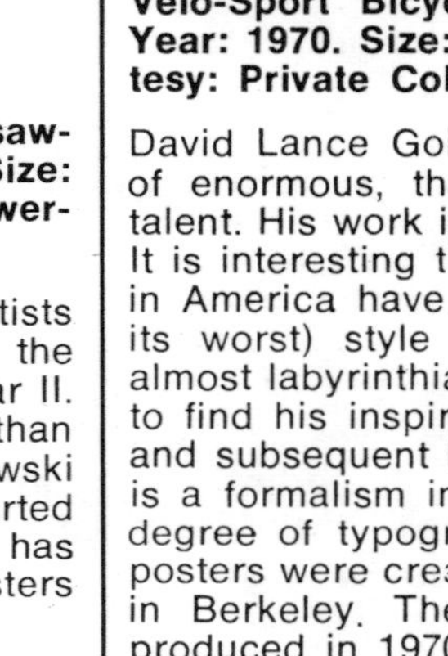

108

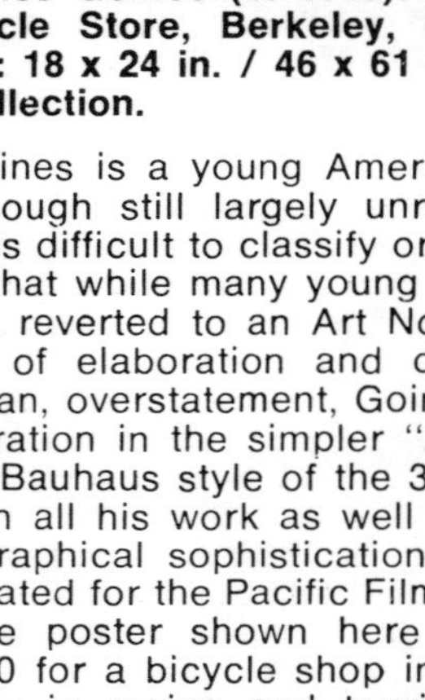

109

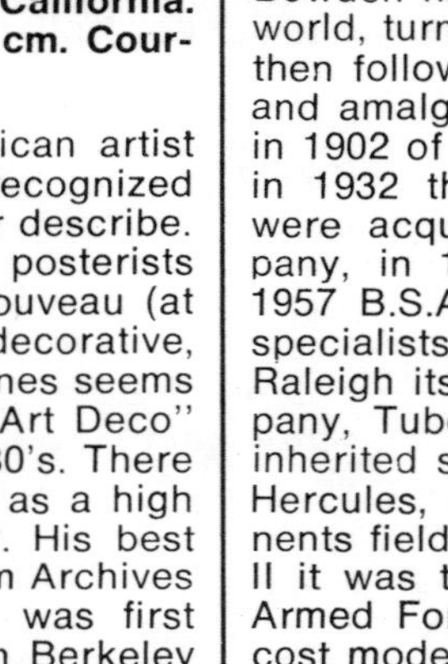

110

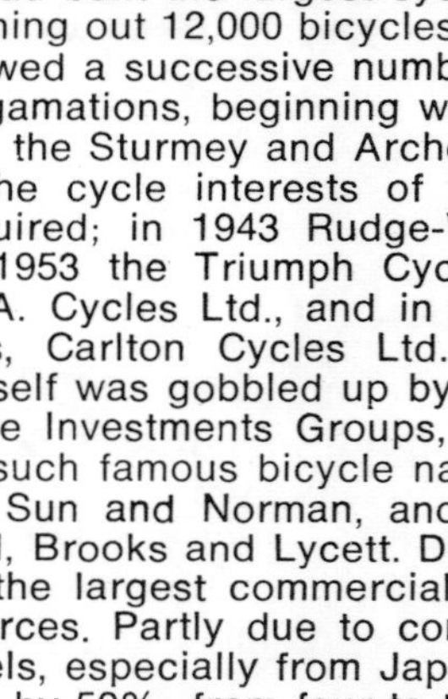

111

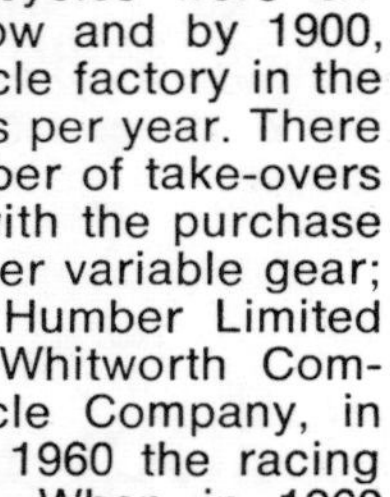

112

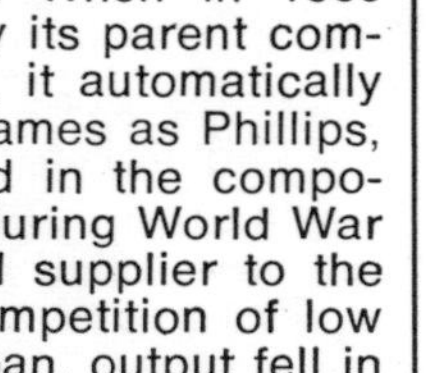

Acknowledgements

I would like to be able to mention the many individuals, companies, and institutions who have been helpful to me in gathering information and materials for this book. I am forced to make the usual apology of insufficient space to mention them all by name, but, at the risk of omitting some and yet hopefully not offending any, I want to single out a few.

First and foremost, our editor, Miss Angela Freytag, working untiringly in doing research in New York and in Germany. After writing over 800 letters to bicycle companies around the world, she followed up by visits to many firms, both in the United States and Europe. While her experiences and reports will make good reading in another, more lively book, they proved also most helpful to me in producing this one. Angela, you're beautiful.

My friend Mr. Michel Romand of Galerie Documents once again made his poster collection and poster knowledge — both of which are among the most extensive in the world — open to me; anyone interested in posters should not miss a visit to this Gallery in the Rue de Seine, in the heart of Paris' most charming "quartier."

As previously indicated, all posters shown here were photographed from the originals, and I would like to express my gratitude to the photographers who did such excellent work, often under inadequate museum conditions: Mr. J. Sardi of Atelier d'Art de Paris, whose fine craftsmanship is only equalled by his kindness and enthusiasm; Mr. R. Lalance, also of Paris; Mr Ton Teuben of the Fotostudio Ton Teuben of Heerenveen, Holland; Miss Barbara Davatz of Zurich, the world's most beautiful photographer, and a fine one, at that; Mr. Davis of the Library of Congress's studio, Washington.

One photographer whose friendship since the beginning of this project I much prize, and whose generosity, patience and cheerfulness in the face of outrageous demands remain a mystery to me, is Mr. Hasso Bruse of Korb, a faculty member of the Staatliche Akademie der Bildenden Kunste of Stuttgart.

The help of the various museums has been in every case quite encouraging and enthusiastically given. It has been a rare privilege and source of much inspiration to me to have spent time with these knowledgeable individuals who have so freely given of their time and expertise. I would especially like to single out Mr. Peter Obermuller, Curator of Prints, of the Kunstgewerbemuseum in Zurich, and Mr K. Wobmann, Curator of the impressive poster collection there, whose cataloguing and storing of posters should set an example for other museums to follow; Mr. Jean Adhémar, Director of the Print Department, and especially Mr. Charles Pérussaux, Curator of the Poster Collection, both of the Bibliothèque Nationale in Paris, who made what must be the largest and certainly one of the most fabulous poster collections in the world freely available to me and made my visits to the subterranean poster vaults of the Bibliothèque such delightful experiences; Madame G. Picon, Chief Curator, and her staff, at the Bibliothèque des Arts Décoratifs of the Musée des Arts Décoratifs in Paris; Mr. H. Hiensch of the Bicycle Museum of the Batavus firm in Heerenveen, Holland, whose fine collection, both of posters and bicycles, is further acknowledged in my comments to 74 above; Mr. Graham Reynolds, Keeper of the Department of Prints & Drawings, and his associate, Mr. Dickenson, at the Victoria & Albert Museum, London. Also helpful were Dr. Heinrich Geissler, Head of the Print Department of the Staatsgalerie Baden-Württemberg, Stuttgart; Mrs. Elena G. Millie, Curator of Posters at the Library of Congress, Washington; Mr. Sandy Burr, of the Sandy-Val Graphics Collection, New York. To these and all other museums, collectors and companies who were so helpful and who gave us permission to photograph and reproduce these posters, my gratitude for making this book possible.

I would also like to express my thanks to Miss Vivien Rowan, Mr. Bernard Jacobson, Mr. Yoshi Nishikawa, Mr. R. E. Fluddy, Mr. Robert E. MacNair, Mr. Ernst Lurker, Mrs. Helen Bollag, Mr. William B. Laighton, Jr., Miss Dorothy Mozley, and also to the staff of the Bicycle Institute of America. Thanks also to the many individuals at the bicycle companies who responded to our requests for posters and information, even the majority who sadly indicated they had no posters to send us, some for good reasons ("We have no old posters available, owing to the fact that the greater part of our files got lost during World War II" —Gazelle, Holland) and some for not-such-good reasons ("It would have been a pleasure to help you with some posters, but unfortunately advertisements on TV, Radio and Press have made posters unnecessary." — Beistegui Hermanos, S.A., Spain).

In the production of this book, I have had the assistance of our fine designer, Mr. Harry Chester and his staff, of Mr. Sandro Diani and the staff of Scala, and of Mr. Andrew Merson, of MacNaughton Lithograph, a good friend and a good printer. This is the first book that I have been privileged to produce for the firm of Harper & Row, the encouragement I have received from their staff, but especially from Mr. Cass Canfield, Jr., makes me hope that this will be the first of many.

And finally, if I had the space to properly devote a full page for a dedication, I would have to dedicate this book to my wife Charlotte, whose endurance and understanding of all my foibles and sicknesses, most notably my acute posteritis, has been beyond the call of wifely duty and remains a marvel that sustains me.

Jack Rennert
President, Darien House, Inc.
New York City, June 1973

Bibliography

Since this book is not meant as a scholarly or complete look at either poster history or bicycle history, no listing of the many reference works in this area need be given here. Let me, however, list a few books not so much because I relied on them in putting this book together — which I did — but because I can wholeheartedly recommend them as enjoyable reading.

To those interested in poster art, there is the first "bible" of the trade, which is hard to come by, Ernest Maindon's *Les Affiches illustrées* (Paris, 1896; an edition of 1,025 copies, in French only.) Easier to locate are Bevis Hillier's *Posters* (London: Weidenfeld & Nicolson Ltd.; New York: Stein & Day, 1969), a delightfully written book that covers the whole history of posters and shows the writer's unique grasp of the subject and flair for writing that is as engaging as it is informative; Lady Jane Abdy's book, *The French Poster* (London: Studio Vista; New York: Clarkson N. Potter, 1970), shows the writer's intimate knowledge of the French masters from Chéret to Cappiello and is written with insight and warmth. For pure visual delight, I would recommend Hillier's *100 Years of Posters* (London: Pall Mall Press; New York: Harper & Row, 1972); Hermann Schardt's *Paris 1900* (London: Thames & Hudson; New York: G. P. Putnam's Sons, 1970); and a very difficult one to locate, except in a few libraries, the five volumes of *Les Maîtres de l'Affiche* by Roger-Marx (Paris, 1896-1900).

There have been over 100 books on the subject of bicycles published in the United States in the last three years alone; almost all of them are practical how-to books — how-to buy, how-to repair, how-to ride in the city, how-to ride in the country. I expect any day to find a book by an enterprising publisher that will tell us *How to Make Love on a Bicycle*, subtitled, of course, *Sex on Cycles*. What another enterprising publisher might do is to bring out a single book that will give the entire history — technical, social, cultural, military, economic — of the bicycle throughout the world, from its beginnings to today. There is no such book on the market, but as an aid to a prospective author, I would recommend that he first contact three writers whose works I have enjoyed reading: Robert A. Smith, author of *A Social History of the Bicycle* (New York: American Heritage Press, 1972), which looks at America's earlier infatuation with the bicycle at the turn of the century (and don't let the footnotes scare you, it's delightful and easy to read); and two British authors, John Woodforde (*The Story of the Bicycle.* London: Routledge & Kegan Paul Ltd.; New York: Universe Books, 1970) and Frederick Alderson (*Bicycling: A History.* England: David & Charles; New York: Praeger Publishers, 1972). These two books concentrate largely on the English scene and the emphasis is on pre-World War I bicycle history. Alderson's is the more comprehensive guide.

The author should then contact three other individuals who have not written books but who would provide key chapters to this international review. Mr. G. Reimer of Drieberge, Holland, at 83, is an expert on both bicycles and automobile history, having started an auto museum and an auto mechanics school. Mr. René Geslin's continuing series of articles on the history of the bicycle that appear in his magazine, *Le Cycle,* add much to the technical and historic aspects of the bicycle, although admittedly with a French bias. (These are not as stridently nationalistic as some earlier works, however, such as the 1938 French book, *Le Vélo,* appropriately subtitled *Fils de France,* in which the authors not only show understandable pride in the contribution of the French inventor Michaux, but go on to take credit for the invention of every single bicycle component, ending with a rousing claim that to France belongs the credit for the invention of the airplane as well, since the Wright brothers, two bicycle mechanics from Dayton, Ohio, used a motor that, they claim, was a reproduction of one manufactured by the French motorcycle and bicycle firm of Darracq!). Finally, Mr. Gerd Volke, of the firm of Jung & Volke, Düsseldorf, Germany, has archives and a museum, as well as personal knowledge, that would give such book much authority and, especially, great details on the history of the German and Austrian bicycle industry. I would especially like to indicate my debt to Mr. Riemer, Mr. Geslin and Mr. Volke for their personal help and enthusiasm on this project. Now, if one could only gather together these six men along with a firm, multi-lingual, global-viewing editor, perhaps there would emerge a truly international source book on the history of the bicycle.

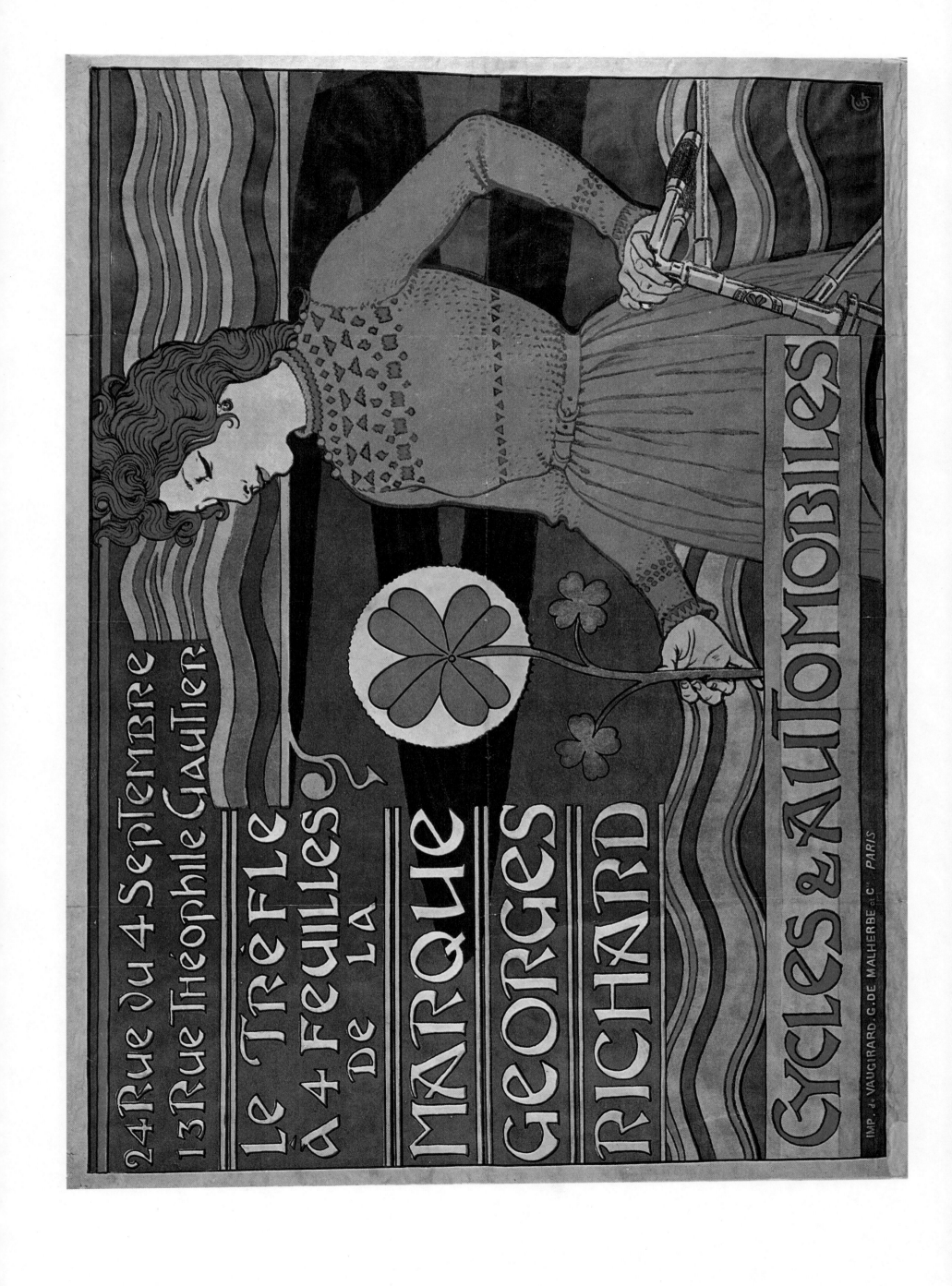

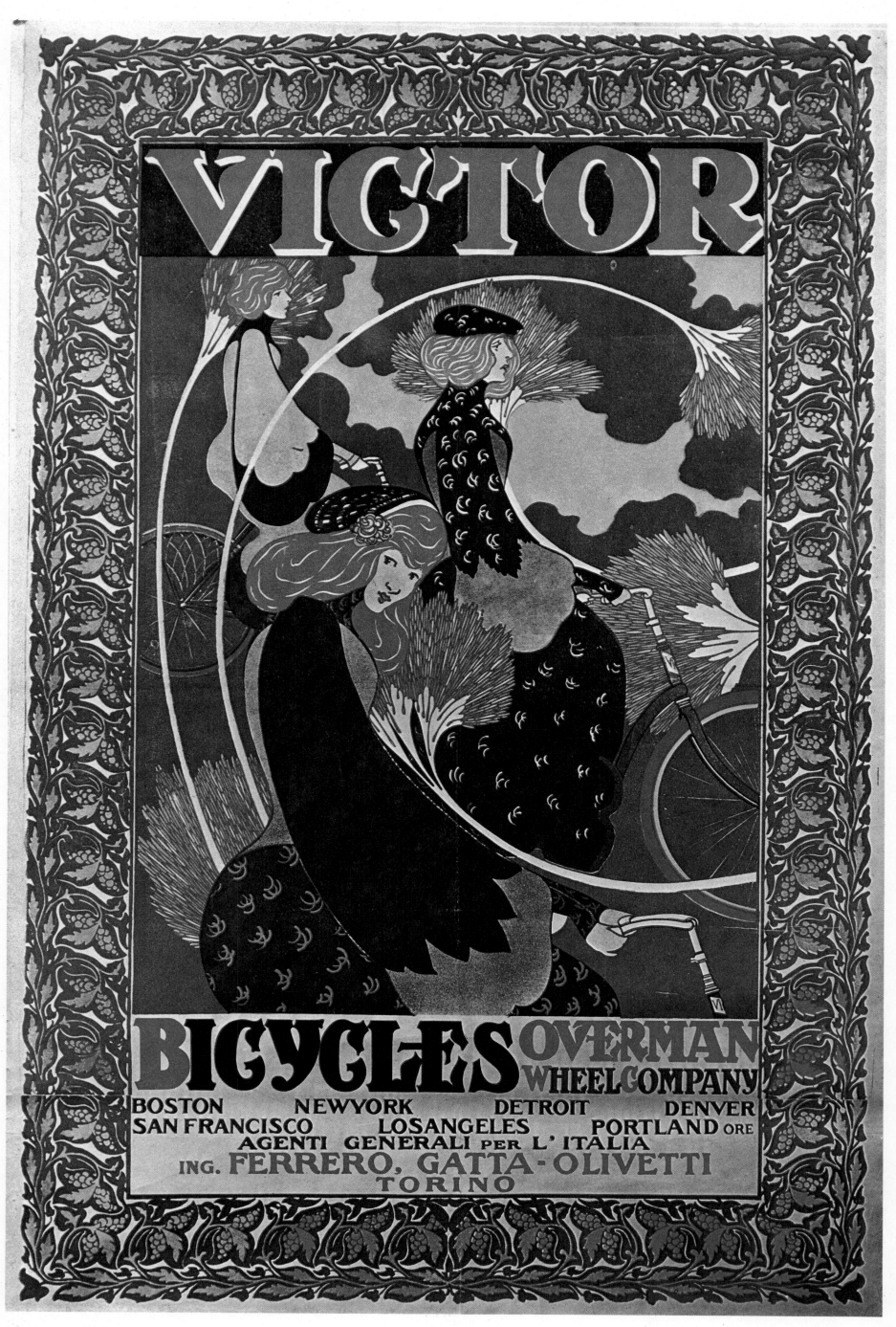

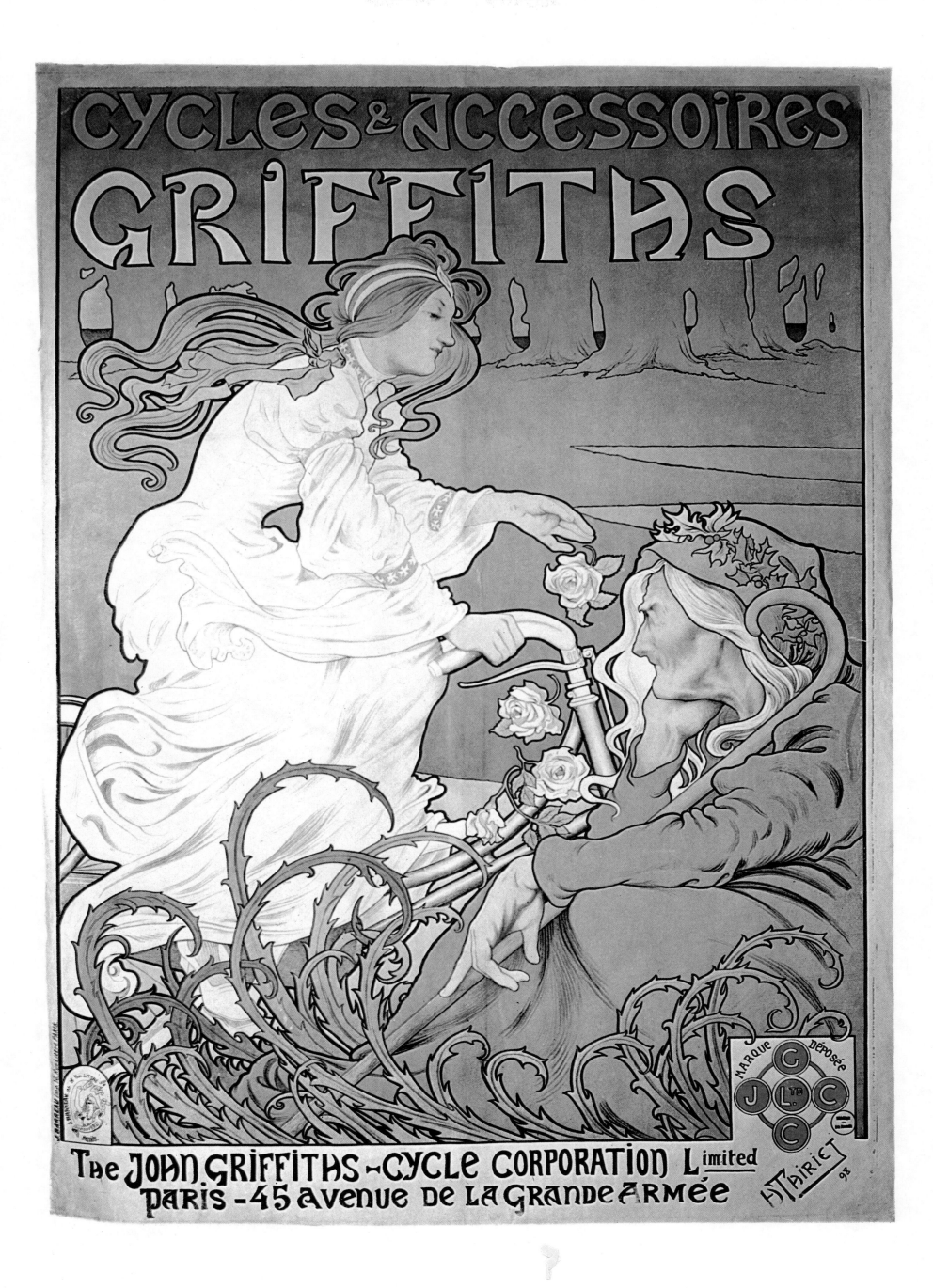

Imp. CHARLES VERNEAU, 114, Rue Oberkampf, PARIS

AFF. D'ART O. DE RYCKER & MENDEL BRUXELLES

RÉPUBLIQUE FRANÇAISE

VILLE DU PARC SAINT-MAUR

LE DIMANCHE 27 SEPTEMBRE 1885, A UNE HEURE

SUR LA PLACE DES TILLEULS

GRANDES COURSES

DE

BICYCLES ET DE TRICYCLES

Organisées par la

Société Vélocipédique du Parc Saint-Maur

Avec le Concours des

SOCIÉTÉS VÉLOCIPÉDIQUES DE PARIS

Et des Champions de France : MM. De CIVRY, DUBOIS, J. TERRONT

PROGRAMME DES COURSES

= Défilé général à 1 heure. = (*Distances : 4 tours, soit 2.800 mètres.*) = Courses à 1 heure 1 2 =

COURSE des AMATEURS
(*Bicycles*)

1ʳ Prix Méd. Vermeil
2ᵉ Prix Diplôme
3ᵉ Prix Diplôme

COURSE des JUNIORS
(*Bicycles*)

1ʳ Prix 30 francs
2ᵉ Prix 25 francs
3ᵉ Prix 20 francs

COURSE INTERNATIONᴸᴱ
(*Bicycles*)

1ʳ Prix 50 francs
2ᵉ Prix 30 francs
3ᵉ Prix 20 francs

COURSE de la SOCIÉTÉ
(*Tricycles*)

1ʳ Prix Méd. Vermeil
2ᵉ Prix Médaille Argent
3ᵉ Prix Médaille Argent

COURSE du HANDICAP
(*Bicycles*)

1ʳ Prix 30 francs
2ᵉ Prix 25 francs
3ᵉ Prix 20 francs

COURSE des AMATEURS
(*Tricycles*)

1ʳ Prix Méd. Vermeil
2ᵉ Prix Médaille Argent
3ᵉ Prix Médaille Argent

COURSE de CONSOLATION
(*Bicycles*)

1ʳ Prix 20 francs
2ᵉ Prix 15 francs
3ᵉ Prix 10 francs

CONCOURS D'ADRESSE
ET DE VOLTIGE

1ʳ Prix 20 francs
2ᵉ Prix 15 francs
3ᵉ Prix 10 francs

La Distribution des Prix aura lieu à la Tribune du Jury

RÈGLEMENT

Le Costume de Courses et la Toque sont de rigueur, sauf pour les Amateurs.
Le Directeur des Courses aura le droit d'éliminer les Coureurs dont la tenue ne serait pas convenable.

Les règlements en usage dans les Courses seront appliqués à cette tournée.
Un Local spécial sera mis à la disposition des Coureurs.

Pendant toute la durée des Courses, un Concert sera donné par l'excellent Orchestre de M. ARTUS

Le Président de la Société
Vᵉ ANDRÉ

Les Membres du Comité :
COSTES, QUENTIER, MARION, THIBAULT
MARTIN, COSTER, JACQUIER, ROUSSEAU, J. TERRONT

Le Maire,
PIETTRE

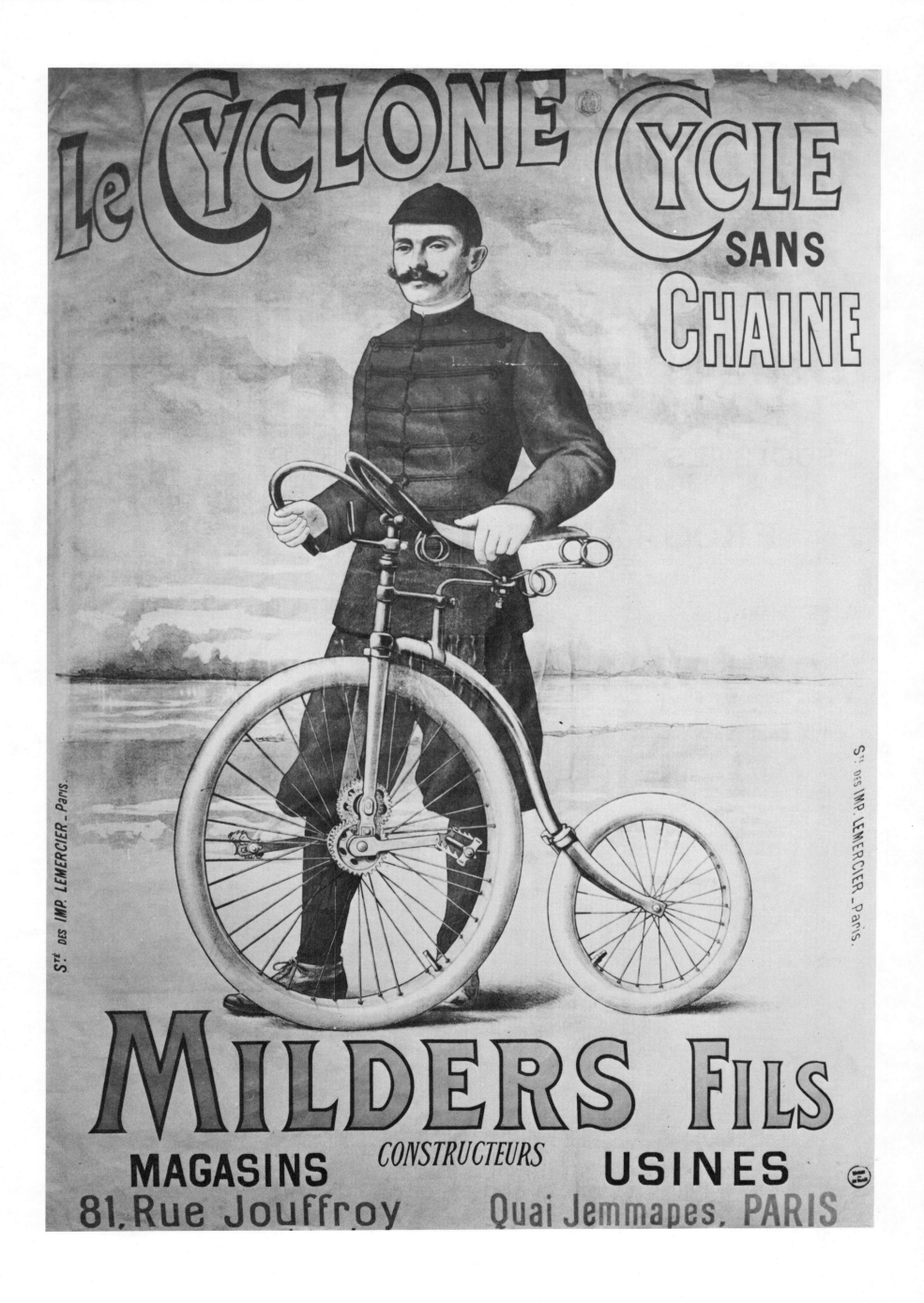

SURREY Bicycle Club SPRING·RACE·MEETING Under N.C.U. rules KENNINGTON OVAL SATURDAY, APRIL 20 1895.

Commencing at THREE P.M

TEN MILES SCRATCH RACE FOR 50 GUINEAS CHALLENGE CUP

ONE MILE HANDICAP

HALF MILE SCRATCH RACE FOR SYDNEY TROPHY

ONE MILE SCRATCH TANDEM BICYCLE RACE

— BANDS —

OF THE ROYAL ARTILLERY AND THE 4TH V B EAST SURREY REGIMENT BY KIND PERMISSION OF THE COMMANDING OFFICERS

FRANK CHESWORTH /95

ADMISSION - - ONE SHILLING
HALF-PRICE IF PURCHASED BEFORE THE DAY.

RESERVED COVERED STAND TICKETS 1/- EXTRA.

To be obtained on the Grounds on DAY OF RACES ONLY, or of the Hon. Secretary, A. R. LOCKWOOD, Surrey Bicycle Club, 57/8 CHANCERY LANE, W.C.

ADMISSION TICKETS may be obtained of the Hon. Sec., 57/8 CHANCERY LANE, W.C.; or of the following

NEWINGTON	H. Wirbatz, 18a, New Kent Road.	CITY	Marriott and Cooper, 1, Holborn Viaduct.
"	E. Maguire, 556, Old Kent Road.	"	George Norris, 62, King William Street.
KENNINGTON	H. E. Pearce, Newsagent, &c., Kennington Cross.	"	28 and 29, St. Swithin's Lane.
"	B. J. Lockwood, Cigar Stores, 2, Harleyford Road.	"	39, Bishopsgate Street.
"	A. Burrell, 162, Lower Kennington Lane.	WEST END	New Ormonde Cycle Co., 79, Wells Street, Oxford Street, W.
"	J. Douglas & Son, Cycle Agents, 30, Kennington Park Road.	"	Premier Cycle Co., Ld., 34, Shaftesbury Avenue, W.
"	E. J. Kerridge, " Beehive," Durham St., Vauxhall.	"	133, Hammersmith Rd., W.
PECKHAM	R. E. Knight, South London Cycle Agency, 190, Rye Lane.	"	Pansetti Bros., 72, Charing Cross Road.
WANDSWORTH	E. Salkeld, 507, Wandsworth Road.	"	W. J. Coppen, Premier Cycle Co., 5, Lisle Street, Leicester Square.
CLAPHAM JUNCTION	E. J. Fisher & Sons, Webb's Rd. & 110, Falcon Rd.	CAMBERWELL	J. Perks, 41, St. Martin's Lane, W.C.
HOLBORN	F. J. Vant, Cyclist Tailor, 67 & 69, Chancery Lane.	"	R. Briden, 330, Camberwell New Road.
"	A. W. Gamage, Cyclists' Outfitter, 118-128, Holborn.	BOROUGH	J. S. Smith & Co., Indiarubber Manufacturers, 244, Borough High Street.
HOLBORN VIADUCT	C. J. Kirby, Quadrant Cycle Depot, 119, Newgate St.	BATTERSEA	J. Thompson, Bookseller and Tobacconist, 138, Battersea Park Road.
"	Premier Cycle Co., Limited, 14, Holborn Viaduct.	BRIXTON	E. Hope, 58 and 234, Railton Road, Herne Hill.
"	George Norris, 8 and 9, Holborn Viaduct.	"	Trigwell & Co., Limited, Regent Cycle Works, Brixton Hill.
ISLINGTON	Pansetta Bros., 287, Upper Street.		

HILDRED & CO ADVERTISING SPECIALISTS, CONTRACTORS & PRINTERS 26 GT JAMES ST. W.C.

PRIZES ON VIEW AT MESSRS. MARRIOTT & COOPERS, I, HOLBORN VIADUCT.

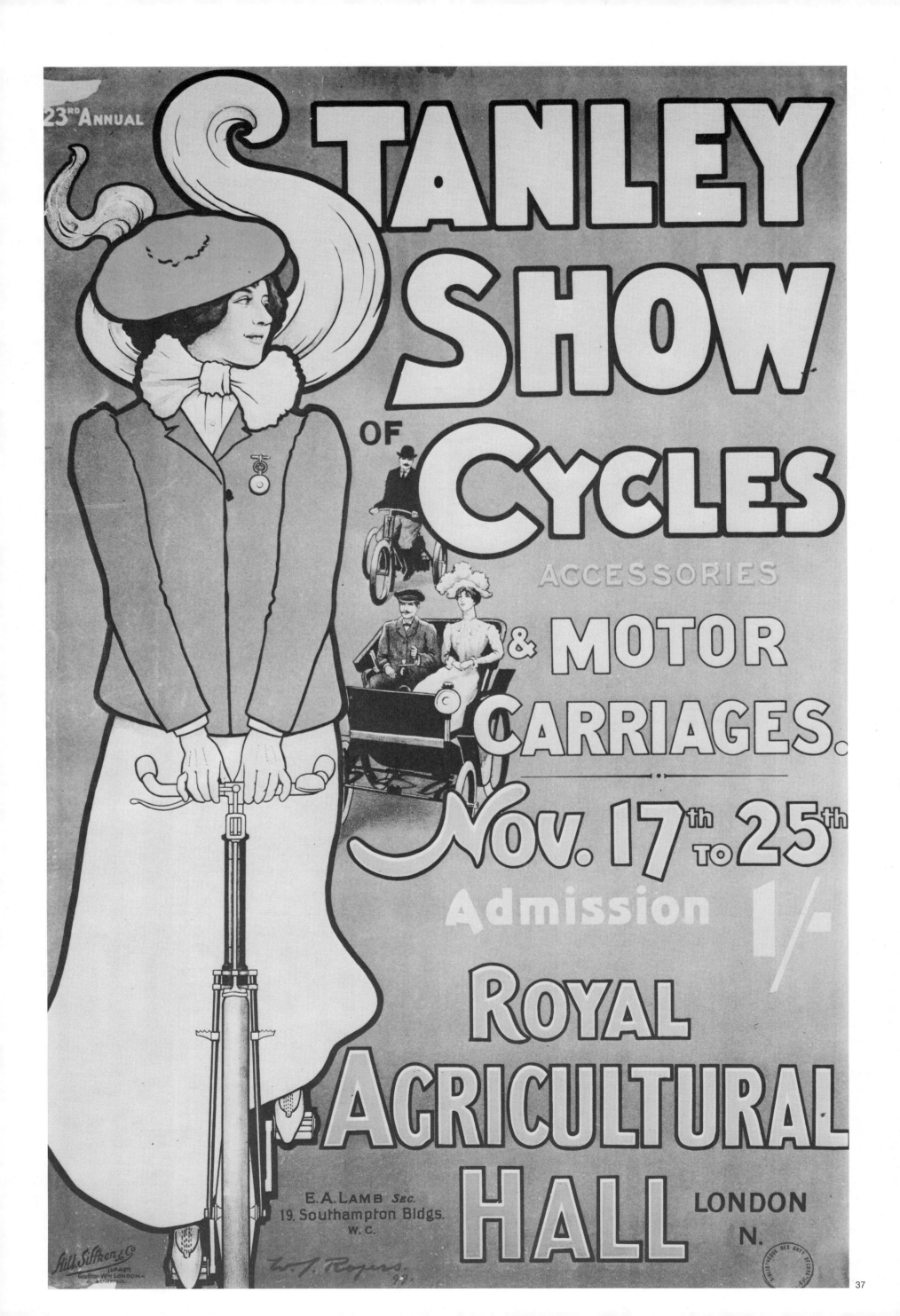

HUMBER & Co L^{TD}
32, HOLBORN VIADUCT. LONDON. E.C.

Imp. G. MASSIAS 17. Passage Daudin · PARIS.

© ATHENA REPRODUCTIONS, LONDON. (TELEPHONE-01234-579) · PRINTED IN ENGLAND. 1980

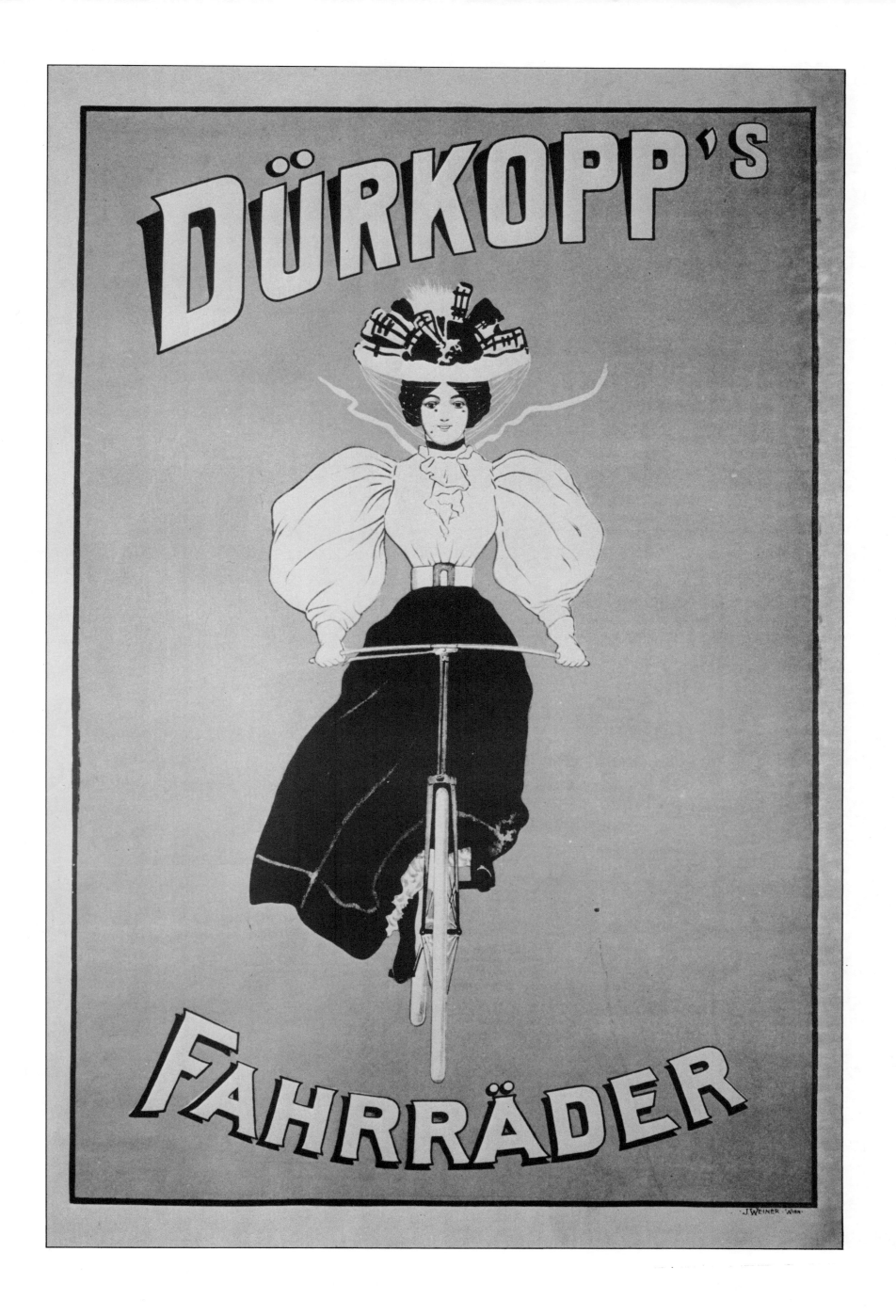

"We are having a heavenly time!"

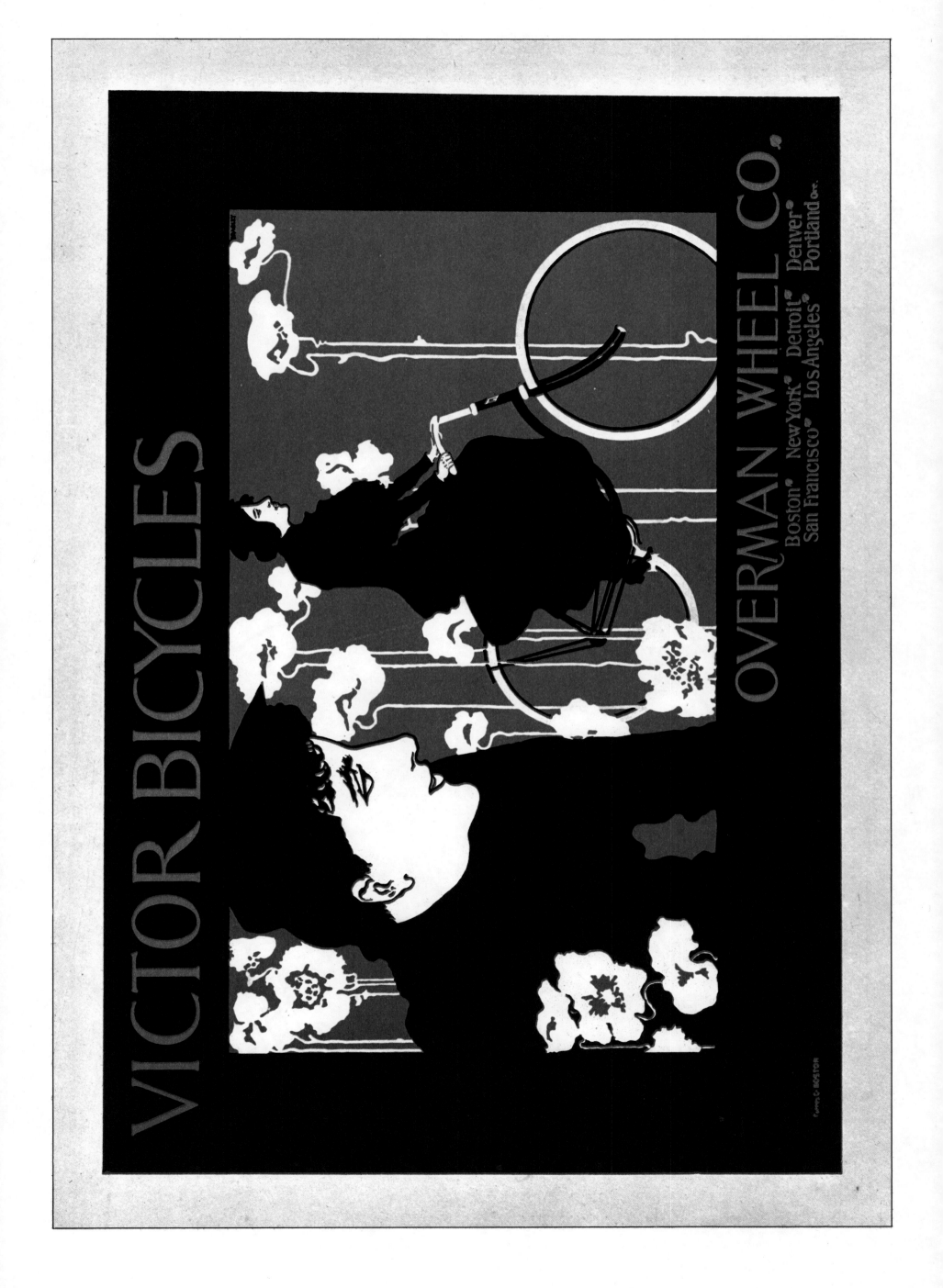

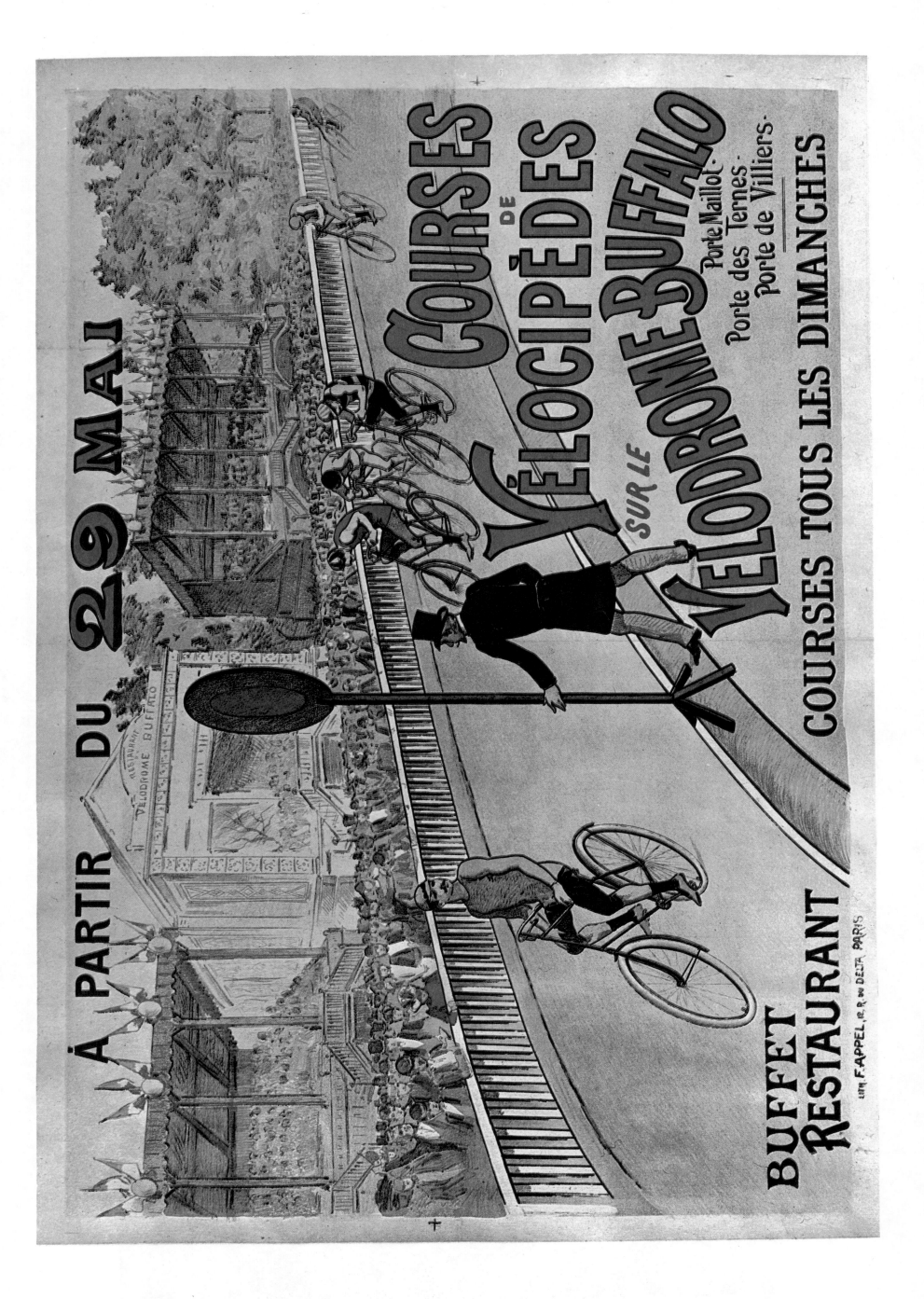

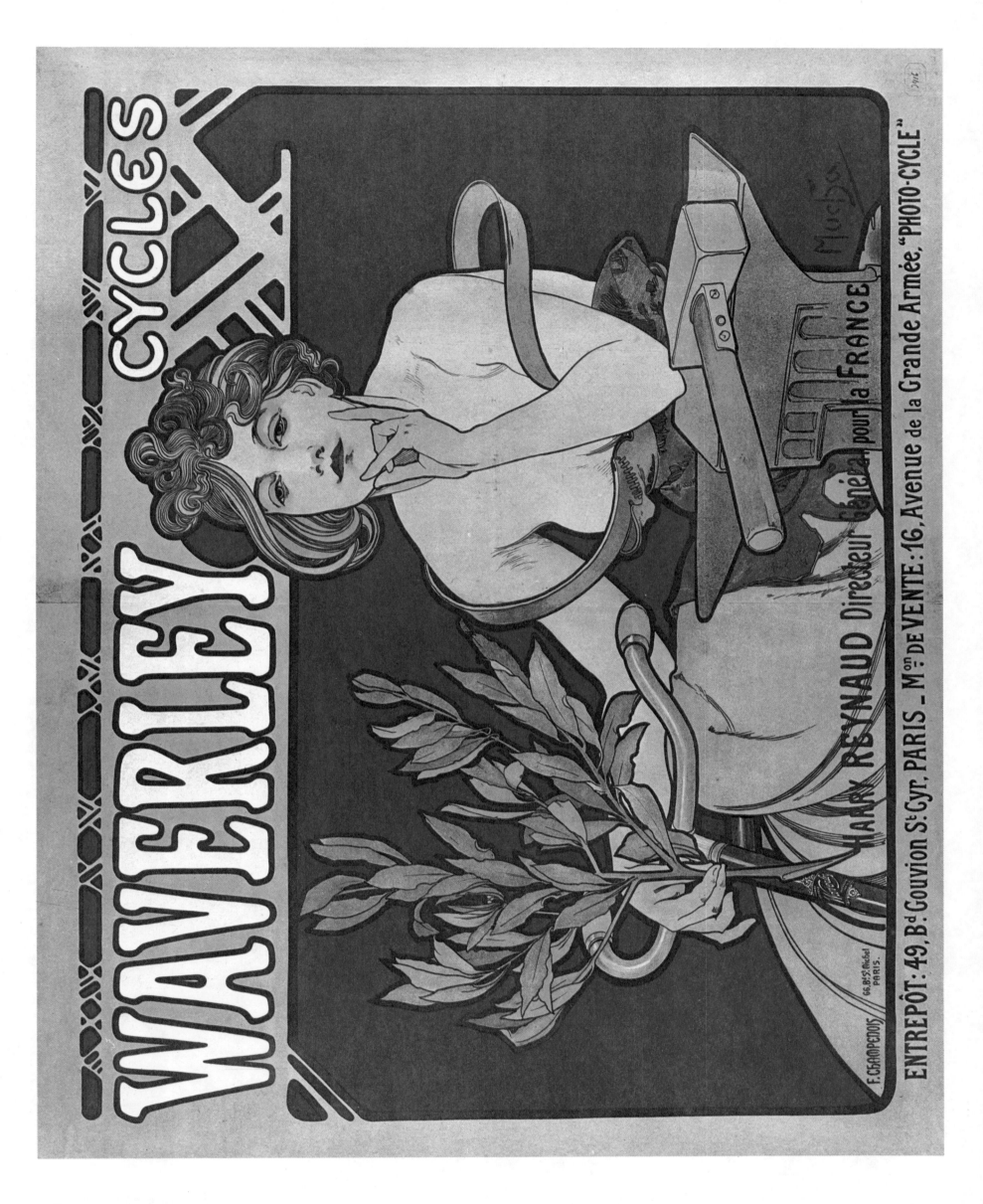

Châlet du Cycle
CHALETS du CYCLE
TELEPHONE
Bois
de Boulogne
LONGCHAMPS
René Péan
IMPRIMERIE CHAIX (Ateliers Chéret) Rue Bergère, 20, Paris. 99.8949 (Encres Lorilleux)

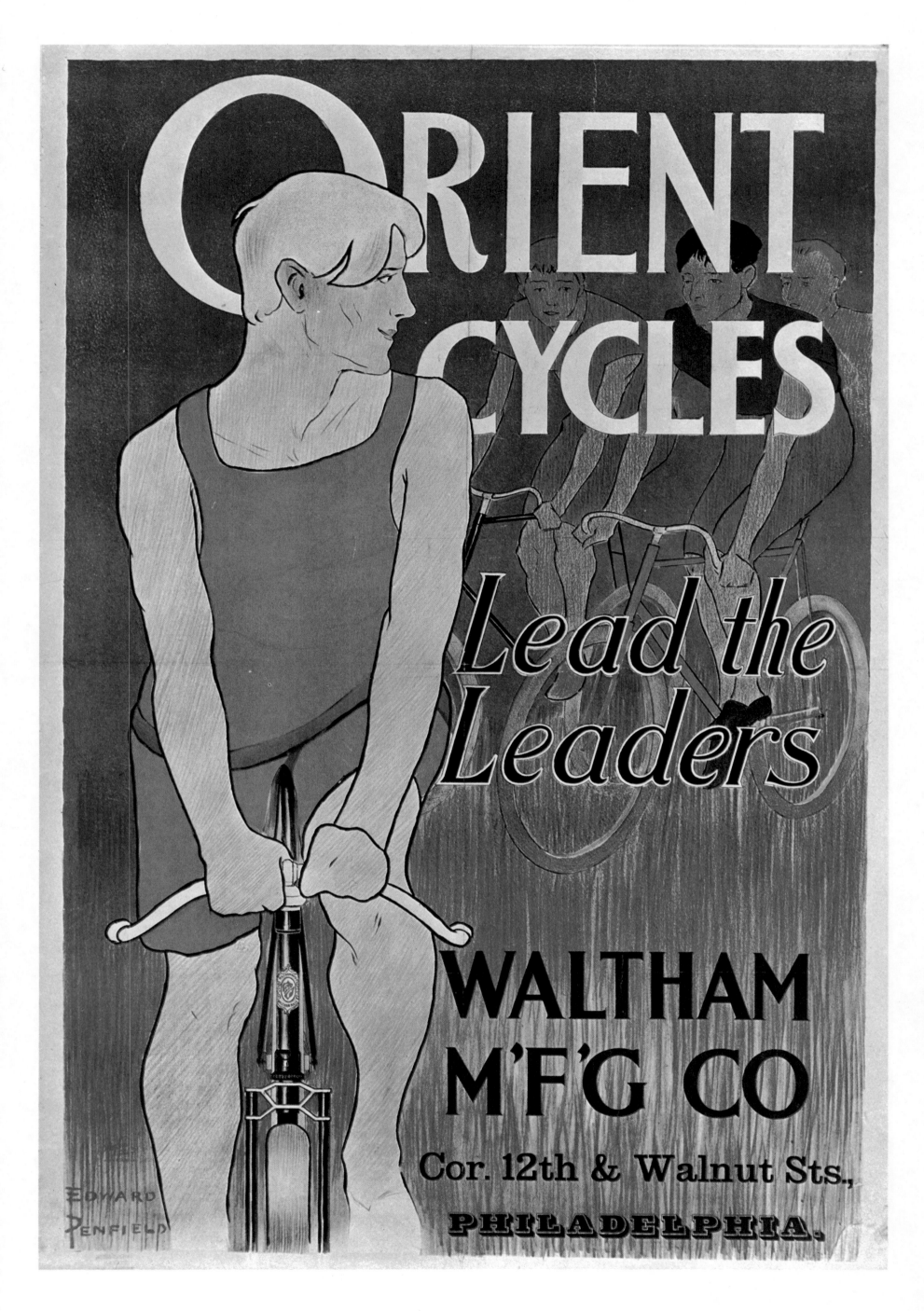

70

FONGERS RYWIELEN. EENIG!

Magazijn:

MIDDELBURG, Lange Delft 19.

RECLAMEATELIER. RÜNCKEL. DEN HAAG.

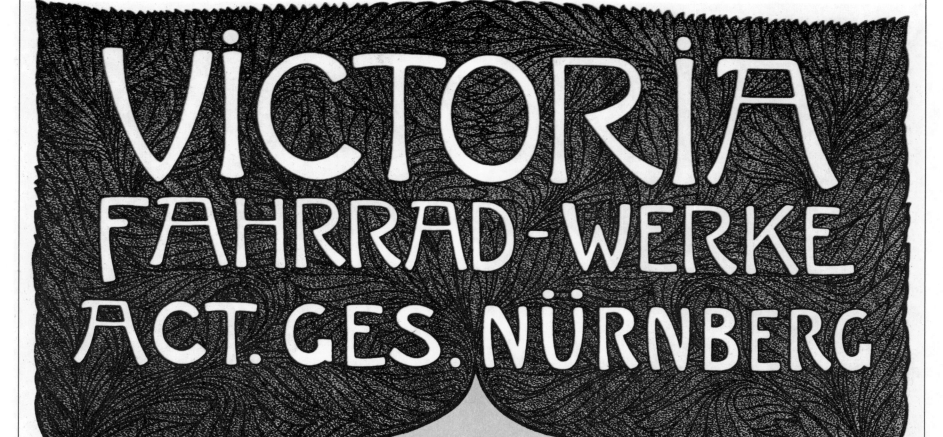

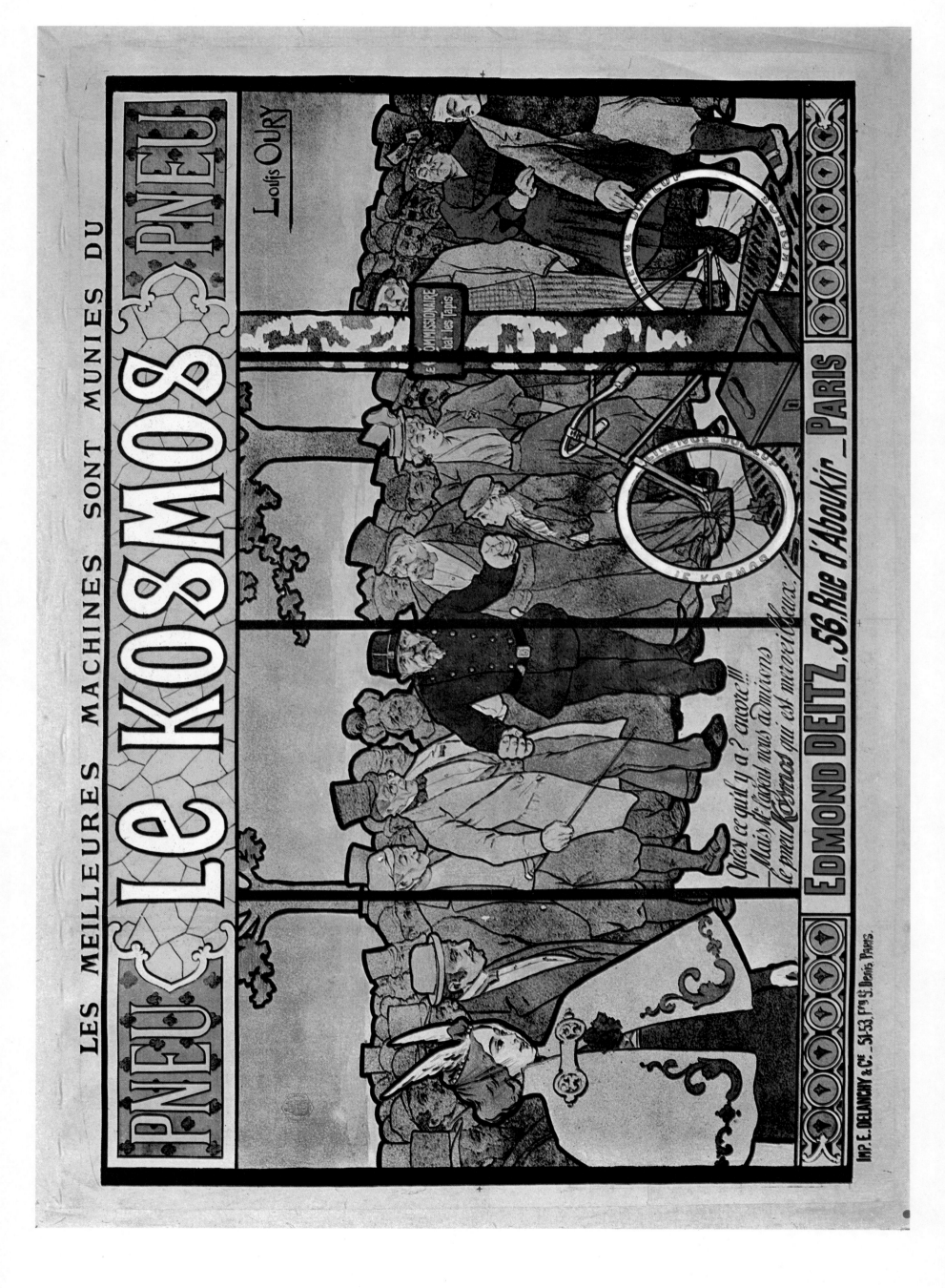

CROWN CYCLES BUILT BY
CROWN CYCLE COMPANY.
LaPorte, Ind.
ARE HIGH CLASS EXCLUSIVELY.

"THE CYCLISTS' CROWN."

COPYRIGHT, 1895.
GIES & CO., BUFFALO, N.Y.

7. BUNDES
FEST

ATB

ARBEITER-
TOURING-
BUND
12.-13. JULI 1947
BASEL
MUSTERMESSE

MEXICO

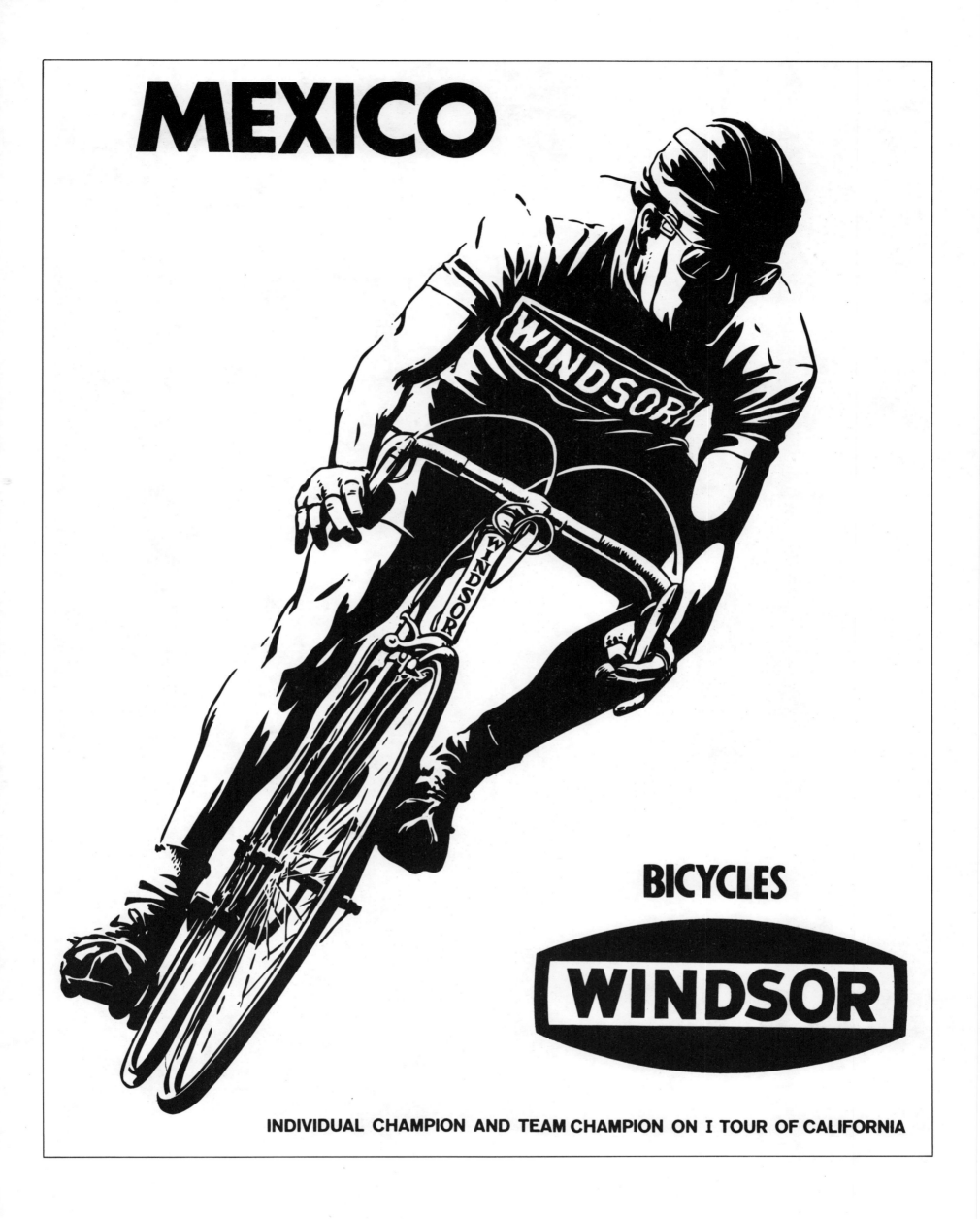

BICYCLES

WINDSOR

INDIVIDUAL CHAMPION AND TEAM CHAMPION ON I TOUR OF CALIFORNIA

創業70周年を迎える　宮田の自転車

株式会社宮田製作所

103

SCHWALBE
c'est un chic vélo

RAD
WELTMEISTERSCHAFTEN
ZÜRICH 22.-26. VIII
LUGANO 29.-30. VIII 1953

XIX
MIĘDZYNARODOWY
KOLARSKI
WYŚCIG POKOJU
PRAHA
WARSZAWA
BERLIN
9 – 25 MAJA 1966
RUDÉ PRÁVO
TRYBUNA LUDU
NEUES DEUTSCHLAND